KONRAD ADENAUER

KONRAD ADENAUER

Edythe Cudlipp

1985
CHELSEA HOUSE PUBLISHERS
NEW YORK

SENIOR EDITOR: William P. Hansen
ASSOCIATE EDITORS: John Haney
                   Richard Mandell
EDITORIAL COORDINATOR: Karyn Gullen Browne
EDITORIAL STAFF: Jennifer Caldwell
               Perry Scott King
               Susan Quist
               Marian W. Taylor
ART DIRECTOR: Susan Lusk
LAYOUT: Irene Friedman
ART ASSISTANTS: Ghila Krajzman
               Carol McDougall
               Tenaz Mehta
PICTURE RESEARCH: Ellen Cibula
               Juliette Dickstein

First Printing

Library of Congress Cataloging in Publication Data

Cudlipp, Edythe.
    Konrad Adenauer.

     (World leaders past & present)
     Bibliography: p.
     Includes index.
     1. Adenauer, Konrad, 1876–1967—Juvenile literature.
2. Heads of state—Germany (West)—Biography—Juvenile
literature.   3. Germany—Politics and government—20th
century—Juvenile literature.   I. Title.   II. Series.
DD259.C83   1985   943.087′092′4 [B] 85-5921
ISBN 0-87754-582-0

Chelsea House Publishers
Harold Steinberg, Chairman & Publisher
Susan Lusk, Vice President
A Division of Chelsea House Educational Communications, Inc.

Chelsea House Publishers
133 Christopher Street
New York, N.Y. 10014

Photos courtesy of AP/Wide World Photos, The Bettmann Archive, and
the German Information Center

Contents

ADENAUER
ALEXANDER THE GREAT
MARK ANTONY
KING ARTHUR
KEMAL ATATÜRK
CLEMENT ATTLEE
BEGIN
BEN GURION
BISMARCK
LEON BLUM
BOLÍVAR
CESARE BORGIA
BRANDT
BREZHNEV
CAESAR
CALVIN
CASTRO
CATHERINE THE GREAT
CHARLEMAGNE
CHIANG KAI-SHEK
CHOU EN-LAI
CHURCHILL
CLEMENCEAU
CLEOPATRA
CORTEZ
CROMWELL
DANTON
DE GAULLE
DE VALERA
DISRAELI
EISENHOWER
ELEANOR OF AQUITAINE
QUEEN ELIZABETH I
FERDINAND AND ISABELLA

FRANCO
FREDERICK THE GREAT
INDIRA GANDHI
GANDHI
GARIBALDI
GENGHIS KHAN
GLADSTONE
HAMMARSKJÖLD
HENRY VIII
HENRY OF NAVARRE
HINDENBURG
HITLER
HO CHI MINH
KING HUSSEIN
IVAN THE TERRIBLE
ANDREW JACKSON
JEFFERSON
JOAN OF ARC
POPE JOHN XXIII
LYNDON JOHNSON
BENITO JUÁREZ
JFK
KENYATTA
KHOMEINI
KHRUSHCHEV
MARTIN LUTHER KING
KISSINGER
LENIN
LINCOLN
LLOYD GEORGE
LOUIS XIV
LUTHER
JUDAS MACCABEUS

MAO
MARY, QUEEN OF SCOTS
GOLDA MEIR
METTERNICH
MUSSOLINI
NAPOLEON
NASSER
NEHRU
NERO
NICHOLAS II
NIXON
NKRUMAH
PERICLES
PERÓN
QADDAFI
ROBESPIERRE
ELEANOR ROOSEVELT
FDR
THEODORE ROOSEVELT
SADAT
SUN YAT-SEN
STALIN
TAMERLAINE
THATCHER
TITO
TROTSKY
TRUDEAU
TRUMAN
QUEEN VICTORIA
WASHINGTON
CHAIM WEIZMANN
WOODROW WILSON
XERXES

Further titles in preparation

ON LEADERSHIP

Arthur M. Schlesinger, jr.

LEADERSHIP, it may be said, is really what makes the world go round. Love no doubt smooths the passage; but love is a private transaction between consenting adults. Leadership is a public transaction with history. The idea of leadership affirms the capacity of individuals to move, inspire and mobilize masses of people so that they act together in pursuit of an end. Sometimes leadership serves good purposes, sometimes bad; but whether the end is benign or evil, great leaders are those men and women who leave their personal stamp on history.

Now, the very concept of leadership implies the proposition that individuals can make a difference. This proposition has never been universally accepted. From classical times to the present day, eminent thinkers have regarded individuals as no more than the agents and pawns of larger forces, whether the gods and goddesses of the ancient world or, in the modern era, race, class, nation, the dialectic, the will of the people, the spirit of the times, history itself. Against such forces, the individual dwindles into insignificance.

So contends the thesis of historical determinism. Tolstoy's great novel *War and Peace* offers a famous statement of the case. Why, Tolstoy asked, did millions of men in the Napoleonic wars, denying their human feelings and their common sense, move back and forth across Europe slaughtering their fellows? "The war," Tolstoy answered, "was bound to happen simply because it was bound to happen." All prior history predetermined it. As for leaders, they, Tolstoy said, "are but the labels that serve to give a name to an end and, like labels, they have the least possible connection with the event." The greater the leader, "the more conspicuous the inevitability and the predestination of every act he commits." The leader, said Tolstoy, is "the slave of history."

Determinism takes many forms. Marxism is the determinism of class, Nazism the determinism of race. But the idea of men and women as the slaves of history runs athwart the deepest human instincts. Rigid determinism abolishes the idea of human freedom—the assumption of free choice that underlies every move we make, every word we speak, every thought we think. It abolishes the idea of human responsibility, since it is manifestly unfair to reward or punish people for actions that are by definition beyond their control. No one can live consistently by any deterministic

7

creed. The Marxist states prove this themselves by their extreme susceptibility to the cult of leadership.

More than that, history refutes the idea that individuals make no difference. In December 1931 a British politician crossing Park Avenue in New York City between 76th and 77th Streets around ten-thirty at night looked in the wrong direction and was knocked down by an automobile—a moment, he later recalled, of a man aghast, a world aglare: "I do not understand why I was not broken like an eggshell or squashed like a gooseberry." Fourteen months later an American politician, sitting in an open car in Miami, Florida, was fired on by an assassin; the man beside him was hit. Those who believe that individuals make no difference to history might well ponder whether the next two decades would have been the same had Mario Contasini's car killed Winston Churchill in 1931 and Giuseppe Zangara's bullet killed Franklin Roosevelt in 1933. Suppose, in addition, that Adolf Hitler had been killed in the street fighting during the Munich *Putsch* of 1923 and that Lenin had died of typhus during the First World War. What would the 20th century be like now?

For better or for worse, individuals do make a difference. "The notion that a people can run itself and its affairs anonymously," wrote the philosopher William James, "is now well known to be the silliest of absurdities. Mankind does nothing save through initiatives on the part of inventors, great or small, and imitation by the rest of us—these are the sole factors in human progress. Individuals of genius show the way, and set the patterns, which common people then adopt and follow."

Leadership, James suggests, means leadership in thought as well as in action. In the long run, leaders in thought may well make the greater difference to the world. But, as Woodrow Wilson once said, "Those only are leaders of men, in the general eye, who lead in action. . . . It is at their hands that new thought gets its translation into the crude language of deeds." Leaders in thought often invent in solitude and obscurity, leaving to later generations the tasks of imitation. Leaders in action—the leaders portrayed in this series—have to be effective in their own time.

And they cannot be effective by themselves. They must act in response to the rhythms of their age. Their genius must be adapted, in a phrase of William James's, "to the receptivities of the moment." Leaders are useless without followers. "There goes the mob," said the French politician hearing a clamor in the streets. "I am their leader. I must follow them." Great leaders turn the inchoate emotions of the mob to purposes of their own. They seize on the opportunities of their time, the hopes, fears, frustrations, crises, potentialities.

8

They succeed when events have prepared the way for them, when the community is waiting to be aroused, when they can provide the clarifying and organizing ideas. Leadership ignites the circuit between the individual and the mass and thereby alters history.

It may alter history for better or for worse. Leaders have been responsible for the most extravagant follies and most monstrous crimes that have beset suffering humanity. They have also been vital in such gains as humanity has made in individual freedom, religious and racial tolerance, social justice and respect for human rights.

There is no sure way to tell in advance who is going to lead for good and who for evil. But a glance at the gallery of men and women in *World Leaders—Past and Present* suggests some useful tests.

One test is this: do leaders lead by force or by persuasion? By command or by consent? Through most of history leadership was exercised by the divine right of authority. The duty of followers was to defer and to obey. "Theirs not to reason why,/ Theirs but to do and die." On occasion, as with the so-called "enlightened despots" of the 18th century in Europe, absolutist leadership was animated by humane purposes. More often, absolutism nourished the passion for domination, land, gold and conquest and resulted in tyranny.

The great revolution of modern times has been the revolution of equality. The idea that all people should be equal in their legal condition has undermined the old structures of authority, hierarchy and deference. The revolution of equality has had two contrary effects on the nature of leadership. For equality, as Alexis de Tocqueville pointed out in his great study *Democracy in America*, might mean equality in servitude as well as equality in freedom.

"I know of only two methods of establishing equality in the political world," Tocqueville wrote. "Rights must be given to every citizen, or none at all to anyone . . . save one, who is the master of all." There was no middle ground "between the sovereignty of all and the absolute power of one man." In his astonishing prediction of 20th-century totalitarian dictatorship, Tocqueville explained how the revolution of equality could lead to the "*Führerprinzip*" and more terrible absolutism than the world had ever known.

But when rights are given to every citizen and the sovereignty of all is established, the problem of leadership takes a new form, becomes more exacting than ever before. It is easy to issue commands and enforce them by the rope and the stake, the concentration camp and the *gulag*. It is much harder to use argument and achievement to overcome opposition and win consent. The Founding Fathers of the United States understood the difficulty. They believed that history had given them the opportunity to decide, as

Alexander Hamilton wrote in the first Federalist Paper, whether men are indeed capable of basing government on "reflection and choice, or whether they are forever destined to depend . . . on accident and force."

Government by reflection and choice called for a new style of leadership and a new quality of followership. It required leaders to be responsive to popular concerns, and it required followers to be active and informed participants in the process. Democracy does not eliminate emotion from politics; sometimes it fosters demagoguery; but it is confident that, as the greatest of democratic leaders put it, you cannot fool all of the people all of the time. It measures leadership by results and retires those who overreach or falter or fail.

It is true that in the long run despots are measured by results too. But they can postpone the day of judgment, sometimes indefinitely, and in the meantime they can do infinite harm. It is also true that democracy is no guarantee of virtue and intelligence in government, for the voice of the people is not necessarily the voice of God. But democracy, by assuring the rights of opposition, offers built-in resistance to the evils inherent in absolutism. As the theologian Reinhold Niebuhr summed it up, "Man's capacity for justice makes democracy possible, but man's inclination to injustice makes democracy necessary."

A second test for leadership is the end for which power is sought. When leaders have as their goal the supremacy of a master race or the promotion of totalitarian revolution or the acquisition and exploitation of colonies or the protection of greed and privilege or the preservation of personal power, it is likely that their leadership will do little to advance the cause of humanity. When their goal is the abolition of slavery, the liberation of women, the enlargement of opportunity for the poor and powerless, the extension of equal rights to racial minorities, the defense of the freedoms of expression and opposition, it is likely that their leadership will increase the sum of human liberty and welfare.

Leaders have done great harm to the world. They have also conferred great benefits. You will find both sorts in this series. Even "good" leaders must be regarded with a certain wariness. Leaders are not demigods; they put on their trousers one leg after another just like ordinary mortals. No leader is infallible, and every leader needs to be reminded of this at regular intervals. Irreverence irritates leaders but is their salvation. Unquestioning submission corrupts leaders and demeans followers. Making a cult of a leader is always a mistake. Fortunately hero worship generates its own antidote. "Every hero," said Emerson, "becomes a bore at last."

The signal benefit the great leaders confer is to embolden the rest of us to live according to our own best selves, to be active, insistent, and resolute in affirming our own sense of things. For great leaders attest to the reality of human freedom against the supposed inevitabilities of history. And they attest to the wisdom and power that may lie within the most unlikely of us, which is why Abraham Lincoln remains the supreme example of great leadership. A great leader, said Emerson, exhibits new possibilities to all humanity. "We feed on genius. . . . Great men exist that there may be greater men."

Great leaders, in short, justify themselves by emancipating and empowering their followers. So humanity struggles to master its destiny, remembering with Alexis de Tocqueville: "It is true that around every man a fatal circle is traced beyond which he cannot pass; but within the wide verge of that circle he is powerful and free; as it is with man, so with communities."

—*New York*

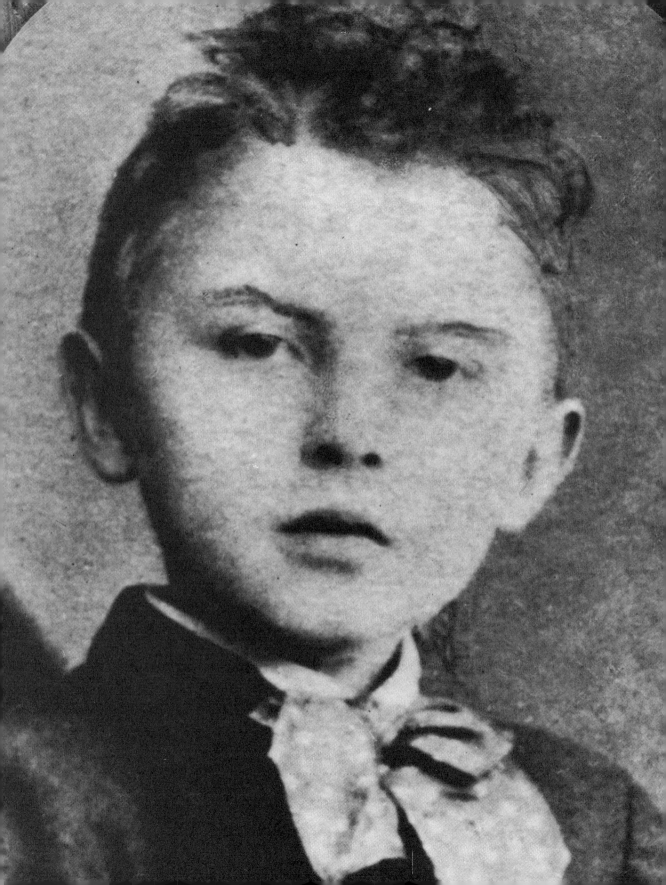

1

A Sense of Duty

Konrad Adenauer, the third of four children and the youngest son, was born on January 5, 1876. Nothing in his family background, his childhood, or even his early adulthood indicated that he was exceptional in any way or marked for greatness. In fact, as the son of a minor government official, he learned early that he would have to work hard to get ahead.

The family of six lived in a small, two-storied house in Cologne, one of the oldest and most beautiful cities in western Germany. Here the elder Adenauer was a court clerk who, although respected, made very little money. To make ends meet, the Adenauers rented out half of the first floor and all of the second floor of their house, crowding themselves into the remaining space on the first floor. The three boys shared one bedroom, and until he was 17 Konrad shared a bed with one of his older brothers.

To add to the family income Konrad's mother sewed oilcloth aprons at home, and when he was five Konrad earned his first money—a penny an apron—by pulling out the basting threads for her. For any luxuries, such as a Christmas tree and the wax candles with which they dressed it, sacrifices had to be made. One year the children agreed to go

Otto von Bismarck (1815–1898), first chancellor of Germany. In 1871, due largely to his efforts, Germany became a unified state under Kaiser Wilhelm I (1797–1888). Shortly before Adenauer was born, Bismarck launched the *Kulturkampf* (cultural struggle), a harsh attack on the Catholic church. Bismarck was a Protestant and a Prussian. His policies caused great resentment in devoutly Catholic Cologne.

Konrad Adenauer (1876–1967) as a boy. The young Adenauer was serious, hardworking, and extremely fond of gardening, a hobby he pursued all his life. His early horticultural career was distinguished by a valiant attempt at crossing a geranium with a pansy to produce "creeper pansies."

Cologne, birthplace of Konrad Adenauer. Situated on the Rhine River, the city is the historic center of German Catholicism. Its cathedral (right), one of the most famous in Europe, has a shrine that Catholics once believed contained relics of the Three Wise Men.

Freiburg University, where Adenauer enrolled as a law student in 1894. After a year at Freiburg, he transferred to the prestigious University of Munich.

without meat for several Sundays to save the money for their tree and candles.

The early habits of hard work and thrift were as much a part of Konrad Adenauer's life as his love of gardening and growing things. Religion was also extremely important.

The Adenauers were devout Catholics who said family prayers every morning and evening. On Sundays the family went to morning Mass and attended evening prayer sessions. When a second daughter died in infancy, the parents' deep religious convictions helped them accept and overcome their painful loss.

Adenauer's father was determined to ensure that his children would have a better life than his own. He was the son of a small bakery owner in Bonn, then a sleepy Rhine River town south of Cologne. He had been orphaned and gained only an elementary school education. After trying several jobs which required no particular skills, he joined the army as a professional soldier, hoping to use it as a stepping-stone to a career in government.

He told his children little of his military career in the Prussian army, except that he had been badly wounded in a war against Austria in 1866. He had been found lying in a pile of dead and wounded at the Battle of Königgrätz, still clutching a captured Austrian flag. His bravery in this battle, the bloodiest in European history up to that time, had won him a commission as a lieutenant, an honor given to only one other enlisted man during that particular conflict. But what might have been a bright military future ended when he fell in love with Helene Scharfenberg, the daughter of a Rhineland bank clerk. Faced with the choice of an army career or Helene, he chose the latter.

The two, though opposites in many ways, were both hot-tempered, quick to argue and just as quick to make up. Helene was lighthearted and easygoing. She liked to sing throughout her difficult working day, never seeming to mind the long hours spent caring for her family and boarders. Konrad was especially attached to her. He also greatly respected his father, who was quiet, strict, and a powerful example of duty, thrift, and religious devotion.

The importance of securing a good education was taken for granted in the Adenauer household. Part of the money the family was able to save

Konrad (at left), his brothers Hans and August, and his sister Lilli, circa 1900. A younger sister, Elisabeth, died of meningitis when Konrad was six.

15

Adenauer spent two happy years studying law in Munich, a bustling commercial and cultural center. His education would normally have been interrupted by compulsory military service when he turned 20, but the army rejected him because of weak lungs.

paid for the three boys' tuition at the Gymnasium, a special preparatory school for potential university students. To give them a head start, the elder Adenauer had sacrificed much of his leisure time to teach the boys himself. As a result they all were able to skip first grade. He also made sure they studied. One day when the sound of fire engines nearby took one of Konrad's brothers from his homework, his father scolded, "Even if guns fire beside you, you have to stay at your work."

Konrad was a good student, always near but never at the top of his class. While other boys played, Konrad could often be found reading. His favorite authors, which he read in translation, were James Fenimore Cooper, an American; Jules Verne, a Frenchman; and Charles Dickens, an Englishman. Though well-liked, Konrad made only one close friend, Ildefons Herwegen, who later became a priest and would eventually play an important role in Adenauer's life.

By the time he graduated from the *Gymnasium* in 1894, Konrad had decided that he wanted to study law at college. Unfortunately, the family's savings had been largely depleted from sending his two older brothers to college. Konrad was thus obliged to begin working life as an apprentice at an old and established Cologne banking firm.

After two weeks of running errands, pouring coffee for clerks, and taking ledgers from the safe, Konrad became depressed. This must have seemed a sad alternative to a higher education. His father, noticing Konrad's unhappiness, took the boy aside and informed him that he had applied to a foundation that gave scholarships to talented boys. If both Konrad and the family were as thrifty as possible, and if the grant actually came through, Konrad could go to the university. That is exactly the way things turned out.

In retrospect, Konrad admitted that the brief experience at the bank had even had a beneficial effect: "I came to realize what it means to a young man to be compelled to accept an uncongenial career. I shall never cease to be grateful to my father for having, from the goodness of his heart, spared me this fate."

Konrad Adenauer lived up to his parents' expectations. In 1894 he became a law student at Freiburg University in Germany's Black Forest region. There he joined a Catholic students' association. Because of his ability to budget money, other students entrusted him with their allowances. He doled out their money as carefully as he did his own, turning a deaf ear to pleas for even a few extra pennies. Adenauer also acquired a measure of fame on the Freiburg campus when he organized a weekend hike of 65 kilometers (about 40 miles) in the Black Forest. Thirteen students started out, but only Konrad and two others finished the marathon—and only Konrad was in class on Monday.

At the university he made one close friend, a fellow law student from northern Germany named

Adenauer and his fiancée, Emma Weyer, in 1902. They married in 1904 and had three children. Adenauer was overcome by grief when Emma died in 1916 after a long illness.

Raymond Schlüter. The two young men were inseparable, attending lectures together and spending their free time walking in the Black Forest. At the end of the year they transferred together to the University of Munich to take advantage of courses better suited to their requirements.

Despite his studies, the years in Munich, the capital of the province of Bavaria in Germany, were probably the most carefree of Adenauer's life. He and Schlüter attended performances at the state-subsidized theater and opera several times each week, and frequently visited the art galleries for which the city remains famous to this day. On holidays they went on walking tours through Switzerland, Austria, and Italy. To save money they did not object to sleeping in railway-station waiting rooms or even barns.

Those two years were the only years when Adenauer willingly lived away from the Rhineland. For the third year of his studies, Adenauer attended the University of Bonn and again Schlüter made the transfer with him. Here Adenauer passed his examinations and was thus permitted to practice as a junior lawyer, though he did not score high enough on his second examination to gain early admission to the Bar itself. In need of money, he took an appointment in the Cologne state prosecutor's office.

For the first time since they met at Freiburg, Adenauer and Schlüter were separated. Schlüter accepted a position at the district court in a nearby town. And a few months later, just before he was to be married, Schlüter died of tuberculosis.

The following spring Adenauer became engaged. He had left the prosecutor's office for a job with a civil lawyer who was also the leader of the Catholic Center party in the Cologne city council. The salary was enough for him to enjoy a social life, and he joined a local tennis club. It was at this establishment that he met Emma Weyer.

The Weyers were an established, upper-middle-class Cologne family, as devoutly Catholic as the Adenauers. Peter Weyer, Emma's grandfather, was the city architect and owned a large art collection. Though Emma's father had died when she was young, her mother was still in mourning for him. Emma had joined the club to escape the gloomy atmosphere at home.

When Emma's conversation became filled with talk of the young lawyer, her brother was instructed to find out more about Adenauer's social standing and professional prospects. Only after Max Weyer discovered that the young lawyer was both ambitious and steady did Emma's mother invite him to the Weyer home. Adenauer's religious devotion and respectable income were the deciding factors to Emma's mother, and Konrad Adenauer and Emma Weyer were engaged to be married in the spring of 1902.

Shortly afterwards Konrad told Emma's brother that what he really wanted in life was to be a notary in a small town in the country, where he could devote himself to his gardening, his inventions, and his family. He received his first patent in 1905 for a new type of steam engine. With his broad knowledge of physics and chemistry he was

Cologne from the north. Cologne lies in the Rhineland, a largely Catholic region of western Germany with strong historical ties to France. The Rhineland was often at odds with Prussia, the powerful Protestant state in eastern Germany. Adenauer's deep attachment to his native city influenced his political views, giving him a more "European," less narrowly "German," outlook.

able to impress his friends and colleagues throughout his life. Emma's brother, who knew of Adenauer's extensive knowledge of plants and gardening, nevertheless hoped that Adenauer did not seriously intend to make his dream of rural existence a reality. Adenauer, however, wanted to be able to support his family from his inventions.

He took a step in the direction of becoming a notary (a public official who oversees and certifies legal transactions) when he changed jobs and became an assistant judge at the Cologne district court. But then, in 1906, two years after he married Emma, he once again considered seeking other employment. He had heard that a post as deputy mayor of Cologne was vacant.

The voters of Cologne elected the city council and they, in turn, elected the lord mayor and the deputy mayors. The civil lawyer for whom Adenauer had once worked was still the leader of the Catholic Center party, which held the majority in the council. In addition, Adenauer's wife had connections to another leading party in the council—the Liberal party.

The Catholic Center party was already considering several other men for the position when Adenauer walked into his former employer's office and asked to be considered. The lawyer liked the

Richard Strauss (1864–1949), the leading German composer of the early 20th century. A court conductor in Munich when Adenauer was a student there, he was at the height of his fame by the time Konrad Adenauer became first deputy mayor of Cologne.

idea and proposed Adenauer to the city council. Adenauer, then only 30 years old, was elected by 35 votes out of 37.

Three days after the election, on March 10, 1906, Adenauer's father died of a stroke. His last words of advice to his son had been: "Now, Konrad, you must aim at becoming lord mayor of Cologne."

In his youth, while Adenauer had been noted for his seriousness and ambition, he had never seemed particularly outstanding in any way. He was obedient, a good student, and well-liked, and had made a few close friends and no enemies. But until he suggested himself as deputy mayor, he did not appear to have any great interest in politics. And yet, it was as deputy mayor that he found his vocation in life. For the next 40 years he would serve his native city, never losing sight of the spires of its famed cathedral.

Before 1815 Germany had been composed of as many as 300 different principalities, each with its own ruler, but by 1815 that number had dropped to 38. But not until 1871, five years before Adenauer's birth, had those states united under *Kaiser* (emperor) Wilhelm I to form a single country. One result of the comparative recency of a unified German nation was that the German people remained for many years greatly attached, on an emotional level, to their respective principalities. Therefore, Adenauer, a man from Cologne, always considered himself a *Kölner*.

Kaiser Wilhelm II (at left; 1859–1941) parades in Berlin with his six sons. Emperor of Germany from 1888 to 1918, he symbolized the Prussian arrogance and militarism that Adenauer hated in German political life.

2
A Prophecy Fulfilled

In 1912 Adenauer was elected to a more important position, that of first deputy mayor, which put him in charge of the city's finances and personnel. In addition, when the lord mayor was away he filled that post too. Since the lord mayor frequently went to Berlin, the capital of Germany, on political business, Adenauer was often responsible for the city's administration.

His responsibilities at home were also growing. After his father's death the young Adenauers had left their apartment in the suburbs and moved into a house closer to the center of the city. They kept the ground floor and the attic for themselves and gave the middle floor to his mother and sister. Emma never complained about the inconvenient arrangement, even after her first son was born in 1906. The child, named Konrad after his father, soon acquired the nickname "Koko."

The birth had been difficult, and Emma was weak for a long time afterwards. A second son, Max, was born in 1910, and a year later the family moved into a larger house. However, after their daughter Ria was born in 1912, Emma Adenauer did not regain her strength. She allowed only her husband to nurse her. He rose early in the morning, came home during his lunch hour, and went to bed late after changing her dressings and taking care of all the other duties of a nurse.

Adenauer as a young man. His appearance changed radically after 1917, when he sustained severe facial injuries in an automobile accident.

Amid all this excitement Adenauer remained absolutely calm and unruffled. That was the first impression I received of Cologne and its lord mayor. During the following months, when I saw him almost daily, it was confirmed and more than confirmed. This man, I felt, was a true commander-in-chief.
—CAPTAIN OTTO SCHWINK
military governor of Cologne in the immediate aftermath of World War I

Adenauer's patent for "Cologne soya-sausage." Adenauer had a lifelong passion for inventions of all sorts. In charge of Cologne's food procurement and distribution during the war, he applied his natural ingenuity to the problem of wartime shortages.

German sailors march into Brussels, Belgium, in 1914, at the outbreak of World War I. Germany entered the war with tremendous enthusiasm, confident of achieving a quick victory by striking at France through neutral Belgium. Adenauer was among the few Germans who thought the war might be a long and bloody one.

When World War I broke out in 1914 Adenauer found himself shouldering more responsibilities than ever. Though because of his weak lungs he had been declared unfit for military service, the hardships of the war increased his work load.

Adenauer did fall ill, however, though the illness had nothing to do with his lungs. He developed a blood clot in his leg. The children were afraid for him, because Adenauer told them that he would die if the clot moved.

When Adenauer recovered he worked harder than ever. He was already well known not only for the amount of work he had already taken on but also for the fact that he seemed always to want to do more. The war offered him that opportunity.

Shortly after the commencement of hostilities he had requested that the municipal food department be placed under his jurisdiction. Anticipating the possibility of food shortages should the war drag on, Adenauer set about making Cologne one of the best-supplied cities in the country, striking deals with local farmers and putting much city-owned land under the plow.

Despite his incredible work load, he also found time for his children, demanding as much of them in school as his father had of him. And the frugality of his childhood had been carried over to the family he headed. As long as the children were neat and clean he paid little attention to what they wore. In fact, he wore his own shoes until the soles were worn through. A city employee who had once been a barber went to the house every two weeks to give both Adenauer and his sons haircuts that were so short, according to his eldest son, that all three looked bald.

In spite of his work load he always found time for his inventions, which were his one extravagance. He was never reluctant to spend money on inventions, whether it was a new kind of automobile, a hairpin, or, during the food shortages which occurred later in the war, "Cologne sausage" and "Cologne bread" made of soy flour or corn. His wife had to wear the hairpins, and the whole family had to eat the sausage and bread.

The only time he relaxed was during the Sunday walks with his children in the mountains overlooking the Rhine River opposite Bonn. As thrifty as ever, he always brought their food and drink

German infantrymen on the move in August 1914. Contrary to expectations, the conflict became the bloodiest in European history up to that time, characterized by bitter trench warfare and mounting casualties on all sides.

from home. His son remarked that when they did stop at an inn no innkeeper ever made any money off them.

In 1916 Emma Adenauer died of kidney failure. Adenauer's mother, who still lived with the family, took charge of the children until Adenauer recovered from his loss. He continued to return home for lunch every day, using the time to talk to his children and listen to their problems.

When one day he did not come home for lunch, the family waited anxiously. In the middle of the afternoon there came a telephone call from a nearby hospital. He had been in an accident. The driver of a car in which he was riding had fallen asleep at the wheel, and the vehicle had crashed into a streetcar. Although the driver had escaped with nothing worse than a few scratches, Adenauer had been thrown against the windshield. When

Das Siebengebirge ("The Seven Mountains"), one of the most picturesque spots along the Rhine. Adenauer often took his children hiking here on Sundays—his one respite from the pressures of war and work.

Tsarist (imperial) troops defend the Winter Palace in Petrograd during the Russian Revolution. In 1917 the Russians overthrew their tsar and established a communist state. In 1918, with Kaiser Wilhelm's armies facing defeat, the radical events of the previous year inspired similar uprisings all over Germany.

somehow he was able to crawl out of the wreckage and stand up, blood was streaming from his injuries. Displaying his habitual determination, Adenauer had managed to walk to the hospital, where he collapsed.

When his family arrived at his bedside, they barely recognized him. The accident had completely changed his looks. Adenauer's nose and cheekbones had been broken, his lower jaw had been crushed, he had lost several teeth, and his eyesight was in danger. So radical was the transformation that in his old age people sometimes mistook Adenauer for an Asian or an American Indian.

After four months in the hospital, he traveled to the Black Forest region to rest and regain his strength. When he had been there a few weeks two members of the city council went to visit him. They casually discussed the war, the weather, and other topics, until Adenauer finally said, "Gentlemen, it's only outwardly that my head is not quite right." The visitors laughed in relief. Adenauer had quickly realized that they had gone to see him to make sure his mind was sound before offering him the post of lord mayor of Cologne.

Soldiers guard Berlin stores to prevent food riots. After 1917, the year Adenauer became lord mayor of Cologne, the war began to go badly for Germany. The army suffered costly defeats, and the civilian population endured great hardship. Discontent mounted steadily, both at home and among the badly demoralized military.

On October l7, 1917, Konrad Adenauer stood in the main salon of the Cologne city hall and took the oath of office. At 41 years old he was the youngest lord mayor of any city in Germany. He must have thought that he had reached the top, for after all, who would have thought that the son of a minor government official could ever become a lord mayor?

Though his eldest son was only 11 years old, the boy recalled one passage of his father's acceptance speech: "There is nothing better life can offer than to allow a man to expend himself fully with all the strength of his mind and soul, and to devote his entire being to creative ability. This field you have opened up for me by electing me lord mayor of the city of Cologne, and for this I thank you from the bottom of my heart."

He needed all that strength and devotion, as well as the creative ability, when the war ended on November 11, 1918. Following the failure of its last great offensive on the Western Front earlier that year, Germany had signed an armistice with Britain and France (whom it had fought since 1914) and the United States, which had entered the conflict in 1917. The first major crisis for Cologne at that time came five days before the armistice. The 1917 communist revolution in Russia had found hundreds of thousands of sympathizers, both military and civilian, in war-torn Germany. Finally sailors in the German navy mutinied, called for a communist revolution, and decided to declare a soviet republic in the Rhineland.

On November 6 Adenauer was informed that a train carrying hundreds of rebel sailors was only hours away from the city. He immediately went to the district military governor to ask for help. The governor refused Adenauer's requests to have the train stopped and its occupants arrested by troops loyal to the government. Just a few hours later a rioting mob was proclaiming a Rhineland communist republic in the shadow of the graceful twin spires of Cologne Cathedral, Germany's finest Gothic church. Everywhere revolutionaries waved red flags and shouted slogans. Some citizens had joined them, but most stayed in their homes or business premises to protect them from looters. Truckloads of armed soldiers rumbled through the streets but did nothing to quell the rioters. Once more, the lord mayor appealed for help, only to be told to manage by himself.

Adenauer was not ready to surrender the historic city with its lovely medieval buildings to a looting, violent mob. He spoke carefully and reasonably to the leaders of the revolutionaries and gained their cooperation. A volunteer civil guard restored a precarious order in the streets. But the elegant city hall was filled with hundreds of people, all wanting to see the lord mayor. Some complained

Helmets become scrap metal after the German surrender on November 11, 1918. The army that had marched so proudly into Belgium four years earlier returned home defeated.

Street fighting in Berlin. During the chaotic winter of 1918–19, revolutionary councils sprang up everywhere in defiance of the Kaiser's government. Due mainly to Adenauer's skillful negotiations with the revolutionaries, Cologne escaped the violence that erupted in many other German cities.

of looting, others demanded bread. Adenauer could not satisfy all of them, but he did what he could. However, he linked some of the army's ineffectiveness to the fact that more than 300 gallons of alcohol had been found in an army storage depot. After dark he had all of it dumped into the Rhine River.

Another crisis was yet to come. Four German army corps had to pass through Cologne on their way home. The vision of hundreds of thousands of armed and hungry men roaming the city and surrounding countryside looking for food and shelter was enough to frighten anyone. Once again Adenauer had to deal with the threat all by himself.

Field kitchens were set up. In addition, before the soldiers could get their discharge papers, pay, and railroad tickets home, they had to turn in their weapons. To pay for all of this, Adenauer gave orders to sell every piece of army property—trucks, cars, horses—to the highest bidder.

Typically, Adenauer set an example by working hard. He also found many conscientious people to help him, often from political parties other than his own. He appealed to their love of their native city, and even if they did not agree with him politically, they did agree that the city came first. These qualities and measures won him the respect and admiration of all who worked with him.

The last German regiment routed through Cologne paraded past the massive doors of the cathedral a few days later. Adenauer watched, tears in his eyes, as the gaunt soldiers in their tattered uniforms marched in orderly ranks across the bridge over the Rhine River.

Three days later, the British army arrived in Cologne as an army of occupation. Adenauer told the commanding officer, "I shall carry out your orders as far as my conscience permits."

"And we," replied the general, "shall treat you correctly as is our duty."

Thomas Mann (1875–1955), Germany's greatest modern novelist, was typical of the German intellectuals who welcomed World War I with patriotic fervor. In 1918 he praised the authoritarian state and the force of "creative irrationality," but he later changed his views and became a supporter of the democratic Weimar Republic.

3

A Time of Turmoil

The quality of life in Cologne had been declining for a considerable period. But during the years after the war Konrad Adenauer reversed this trend and transformed Cologne into one of the foremost cities in Germany. While that would have been an accomplishment at any time, it was almost a miracle during the 1920s. It required all his skills as a politician as well as imagination, careful planning, and hard work. He had to overcome obstacles that would have been too much for most men.

The political situation was a major obstacle for Adenauer. Germany, having been defeated, was in turmoil. Former soldiers and sailors were unemployed, and rampant inflation had rendered Germany's currency worthless—one million marks would not buy a meal in a restaurant. For the first few years after the war, Adenauer could not act without the approval of the British, who had occupied the Rhineland and its industrial plants.

The central government in Berlin was also in confusion. In the last days of the war the Kaiser had given up his throne and fled to neutral Holland. A group of politicians gathered together in Weimar, a quiet city in eastern Germany, to draw up a new constitution and make the country a unified republic—to be known as the Weimar Republic. The central government, however, proved

The victorious Allies meet at the Palace of Versailles in Paris. The Treaty of Versailles, signed on June 28, 1919, blamed Germany for the war, imposed stiff reparations payments, reduced Germany's territory, and slashed its armed forces to 100,000 men.

A Berlin house destroyed by a Spartacist bomb, April 1919. The Spartacists were a communist group that believed President Friedrich Ebert (1871–1925) had betrayed the workers. They were particularly active in Berlin from January to May 1919. At the same time, in the Rhineland, other groups were agitating to make the region a separate state.

President Friedrich Ebert (second from right) presides at a military review in 1919. Ebert, a Social Democrat, faced the difficult task of combatting both left-wing revolutionary elements in his own party and the extreme right-wing groups that blamed his government for Germany's "humiliation" at Versailles in 1919.

inadequate to the tasks it had set itself, and with so many political parties represented, it became apparent that no one man could expect to govern for very long. In addition, Germany had been a nation for less than 50 years and some of the formerly independent states longed to regain their previous status.

As lord mayor of Cologne, Adenauer was in the middle of this disorder. While many people only wanted to hold on to what they had, he saw the time as an opportunity for creative ventures. But since he had to work with the weak national government, the British military governor, and his own city council, the exercising of personal initiative was far from easy. In fact, the city council itself was often his greatest opponent. It was made up of men who held a wide range of political beliefs. Adenauer and a few others were in the middle, but the Communist party members on the left seldom agreed with the very conservative men on the right.

Adenauer had two simple rules for winning

votes to accomplish his goals for rapid change. Firstly, he always did his homework—he went to meetings with briefcases stuffed with facts and figures. Secondly, he always listened, never interrupting. Only when everyone else had finished speaking did he present his side of the argument. Since the meetings often ran until late at night, by which time the councillors were so tired and eager to go home that they would agree to almost anything, Adenauer on more than one occasion purposely brought matters to a vote very late in the proceedings.

While such methods may seem a little devious, it cannot be denied that Cologne grew quite considerably under his tutelage. He built a new harbor on the Rhine River to encourage industry, and brought the American Ford Motor Company and other enterprises to the city. He improved the life of the city's inhabitants by building modern housing and he also built Germany's first sports stadium and 50 other community sports grounds. To improve the quality of cultural life he established the yearly Cologne Trade Fair and opened the world's first Press Exhibition. And he reopened the city's university that had been closed since 1797. Albeit slowly, both Germany and Cologne recovered.

Government soldiers mobilize against the Spartacists in Berlin. By May 1919 Ebert's troops had crushed the rebels. Meanwhile, Adenauer was playing a double game with the Rhineland separatists.

Then, in 1929, just as Germany was nearly on its feet again, a stock market crash in the United States resulted in a worldwide depression which wiped out the recovery. Unemployment soared. Plans which had been drawn up for a national system of four-lane highways laid untouched in drawers in Berlin. Adenauer suggested that the unemployed be used to build them. When Berlin failed to respond, Adenauer simply took matters into his own hands. Between 1929 and 1932 he administered the construction of Germany's first modern highway, which ran from Cologne to Bonn.

An accomplishment of which Adenauer was even more proud was the "Green Belt," a swathe of parkland around central Cologne. Before the war "old" Cologne had been surrounded by a belt of fortifications 25 miles long and two-thirds of a

The Shell Oil Company's refinery in Cologne. In the face of severe shortages and chaotic conditions, Adenauer managed to rebuild Cologne. He attracted many new industries to the city, including several important American firms.

Adenauer displays plans for a "Green Belt" encircling Cologne. After the war the socialists wanted to use this land for housing, the realtors wanted to develop it, but Adenauer fought for a park instead—armed, as usual, with all the facts and figures to support his case.

mile wide. During the war the old fortifications were demolished and the land once again became available for building. As with vacant land in any city, it would soon be quite valuable. Whoever owned it could make a fortune.

Adenauer, however, refused to allow the land to fall into the hands of any more speculators and builders than had already begun dividing up the area between themselves. His first move was to obtain British approval for turning the land into a park. But he still needed permission from the government in Berlin to conduct an expropriation of this magnitude. They agreed and, over the protests of land speculators, passed an ordinance that gave the city control of the entire belt.

Adenauer stuck doggedly to his plans, disregarding all the opposition. He wanted to offer the people an occasional respite from the crowded alleys and streets to which they were accustomed, and he saw the Green Belt as a gift to all the citizens of Cologne. Years later, when Cologne suffered near-total destruction in World War II, Adenauer told his brother-in-law, "The churches are gone but my Green Belt has remained."

Adenauer's appetite for work continued to grow. Even while building and rebuilding Cologne, he was also preoccupied with the broader issues of national politics.

An aerial view of the Green Belt, 1963. The parkland survived heavy bombing during World War II and remained one of Adenauer's proudest achievements.

The concept of an independent Rhineland had gained increasing popularity. The area was rich in coal, which fueled steel mills and other industries. But the loss of the Rhineland almost certainly stood to further weaken an already badly damaged Germany. It is difficult to determine what Adenauer wanted, for he played a double role.

On the one hand, in 1919 he called a meeting of the leading politicians in the Rhineland. He identified himself with the moderate wing of the independence movement, a group that favored making the Rhineland a federated republic within the general constitutional framework of the German state. He even had himself elected chairman of a committee which was to draft such plans as might be necessary for such an undertaking. On the other hand, he never called even one meeting of the committee. Both sides accused him of treason. Those in favor of absolute separation went so far as to pass a sentence of death on Adenauer. The wily lord mayor of Cologne had successfully defused a very dangerous situation by intervening before it became uncontrollable.

In 1919 Adenauer also remarried. The family who lived next door to the Adenauers had two daughters only a few years older than the oldest Adenauer son. The neighbors' eldest girl, Gussi, who greatly enjoyed singing and gardening, suddenly began to make excuses to be in their garden when Adenauer was working in his garden next door, to be outside when his car picked him up in the morning, and to be out after lunch to talk to him. Their discussions were mainly about plants and gardening.

Gussi's parents noticed that the talks became longer and longer. Being Protestants they became upset when Gussi told them that she intended to become a Catholic. Although they liked Adenauer, he was 18 years older than their daughter, who was closer in age to Adenauer's three children than she was to their father. Hoping she would

Adenauer made two trips to Berlin in this aircraft to win government approval for the Green Belt.

Adenauer and his second wife, Gussi Zinsser, at the time of their marriage in 1919. Over the objections of her parents, 24-year-old Gussi converted to Catholicism to marry the 43-year-old lord mayor of Cologne.

forget Adenauer, the parents sent her away to visit relatives, but instead, she returned a few weeks later, declaring that she would never give Adenauer up. After Gussi converted to Catholicism, the two were married. Their first child, born the following year, lived only a few days. Gussi, who had fallen ill during her pregnancy, remained sick for some time after the birth, and was nursed by her sister Lotte and by Adenauer. She fully recovered and together they had four children.

By the mid-1920s Adenauer was known outside Cologne, especially in Berlin. Under the Weimar constitution, voters in the various states, or *Länder*, elected representatives to the *Reichstag*, or general assembly. The *Reichstag* then elected a president whose office was mostly ceremonial. The chancellor, selected by the majority political party, actually ran the government. Unfortunately, this system of government, which had been designed by a brilliant sociologist named Max Weber, had one major drawback. It was, in some ways, almost too representative. There were so many political parties in the *Reichstag*, some with only one member, that no one party was able to secure a working majority that would last.

The various elements of the coalitions that were formed in an attempt to build a majority often had little in common, and they invariably fell apart within months. When this occurred the *Reichstag* would dismiss the chancellor, another man would be chosen, and the president would again ask him to form a government. Until he did, the country had no leader.

By the spring of 1926, 12 different governments had fallen. The leaders of a few of the moderate parties decided to speak to Adenauer and

Workers demonstrate outside the Reichstag in postwar Berlin. Military defeat and the collapse of the imperial government left Germany in turmoil. In 1919 a new constitution established Germany's first democratic regime, the Weimar Republic, but political strife continued.

A 1921 Berlin rally sponsored by the Social Democratic party (SPD). The position of the SPD prevented the formation of stable political alliances during the Weimar Republic. It was too radical for the right-wing parties and for religious moderates like Adenauer, but it was too conservative for the left wing, which held it responsible for mishandling the widespread communist uprisings of 1918–19.

asked him to go to Berlin. Adenauer's support depended mostly on two different parties, both of which were basically Catholic in membership—the German People's party and the Catholic Center party. They did not have a majority, either alone or together, and were weak at the national level. He suggested that they combine and become more broadly based by bringing in Protestants who held similar views. Nothing came of the idea. In the meantime, he needed the support of the Social Democrats (SPD), a leftist party whose members had their roots in the trade union movement.

Adenauer spoke to the leaders of both the Catholic parties and the rival SPD. However, at the end of three days he returned to Cologne. The differences between his supporters and the Social Democrats were too great. He felt that even if he could put together a coalition, ultimately the SPD would ask for too much and undermine the consensus essential to the maintenance of a united front.

If Adenauer had become chancellor the history of Germany might have been different. He had managed to get the different parties in Cologne to work together by appealing to their common love for their city. In Berlin he might have been able to appeal to the patriotism of politicians of all parties. Whether or not he would have been successful, no one will ever know. As it was, there were seven more governments before German democracy fell victim to Adolf Hitler's method of government in 1933.

In 1929 Adenauer was up for reelection as lord mayor. While in 1920 he had been elected unanimously, his determination to have his own way almost destroyed his chances in this election, despite all he had done for Cologne.

There was a raging battle over a new bridge

A German woman burns money for fuel as rampant inflation reaches crisis proportions in 1923. That February, for example, Adenauer was paying 707,364,000 marks (the German currency) for a monthly subscription to a Cologne newspaper. By January 1924, the price was 6,500,000,000 marks.

An anticommunist poster from 1921. The German Communist party was an important factor in the instability of the Weimar Republic. It had considerable support among the workers but was greatly hated and feared by all the moderate and rightist parties.

to be built across the Rhine River. The city council appointed a committee to hold a competition for its design, and as lord mayor Adenauer was on the committee. Seven of the nine judges voted for an arch bridge and Adenauer and one other member voted for a suspension bridge. As usual, Adenauer had prepared all his arguments in advance. The arch bridge, he said, would hide the view of the mountains on the other side of the Rhine, while the suspension bridge would add to the view because of its delicate design.

When the city council did not agree, Adenauer did not give up. He was determined to have a suspension bridge. Although he claimed to hate the communists, his description of the beauty of the suspension bridges in the Soviet city of Leningrad persuaded even them. He had also learned from a city architect that the riverbed might not be able to support an arch bridge. He brought the architect to his office and made him stay until he had written down the facts and figures that supported the argument. Adenauer then had the report presented at the next council. Finally Adenauer won.

However, Adenauer had angered many of his supporters. He was accused of being too high-handed and of running the city as if he owned it. When the time came for reelection, he won by only one vote.

Adenauer remained lord mayor for only three years. As the depression became worse, Germany's problems became greater. The Communist party, representing the workers, became a political threat to the leaders of industry, the right-wing capitalists. The most recent chancellors had been govern-

Adenauer takes part in a procession through Cologne. As lord mayor for 16 years (1917–1933), he guided the city through World War I and its aftermath. Despite his undeniable achievements, many people considered him stubborn, authoritarian, and very high-handed.

An enthusiastic crowd gives the Hitler salute at a 1933 Nazi rally in Berlin. Initially more concerned with the threat of communism, Adenauer soon became alarmed by Hitler's rapid rise to power. From 1932 on, he was a staunch, uncompromising anti-Nazi.

ing by decree, not by law, and generally ignored the proposals emanating from the *Reichstag*. This situation left Germany vulnerable to the advances of would-be dictators, and there was just such a demagogue waiting to take over at that time.

Up until this point the National Socialists, or Nazis, under Adolf Hitler had been a minority party. Because of its tendency to consider violence a legitimate political tool, the party had been outlawed for a time in the early 1920s. But during the depression the Nazis seemed to offer some hope. They were very well-organized and held mass rallies that were impressively staged and often embellished with uniforms, flags, and torch-lit parades. In Hitler and other Nazis the party could boast speakers capable of hypnotizing an audience. Although they were not yet a majority party, the Nazi share of the national vote was increasing, and the party's progress was not entirely due to the intimidation tactics employed by its private army—the Brownshirts. The rabidly racist and nationalistic Adolf Hitler was becoming genuinely popular with the citizens of Germany.

In January 1933 Hitler was appointed chancellor by the president, Paul von Hindenburg. His first act was to dissolve the *Reichstag* and call new elections for March, when he hoped he would get a majority in the newly formed *Reichstag*. The violence and frenzy of the Nazi rallies escalated as Hitler campaigned in city after city across Germany. In February Cologne's time came.

Adenauer did not like Hitler or the Nazis and refused to greet them at the airport. When Hitler landed and saw an expanse of empty tarmac where there should have been a welcoming party, he was deeply offended. Cancelling his scheduled appearance in Cologne, he left for Godesberg where his campaign workers assured him he would find a much more friendly reception.

The Nazis planned to hold a rally in Cologne two days later, and during the night they raised their flags on one of the bridges over the Rhine River. Adenauer ordered the flags taken down since they had been put up without permission. Eventually, the flags were put up at the Trade Fair Hall.

Adenauer's days as lord mayor were numbered. Hitler remembered Adenauer's refusal to meet him, and the local Nazis did not forget the incident of the flags.

Election posters from 1932. During the late 1920s and early 1930s, a series of electoral victories transformed Hitler's Nazi party from a small group of right-wing fanatics to a major political force.

4

Years of Fear

Nazi party organizations and the newspapers in Cologne began a smear campaign against Adenauer in the weeks before the national election. He was accused of wasting the city's money and of being dishonest. When the Nazi Stormtroopers collected money they rattled their collection boxes, calling out, "Every penny a bullet for Adenauer."

Their effort did not go unrewarded. People who had supported him only a few weeks earlier now turned their backs on him. Friends were afraid to be seen with him and also with his family. On the street, the Adenauers were strenuously avoided.

After the national election Stormtroopers were sent to Adenauer's home to live with his family. Although the Nazis claimed that this was simply for his protection, in fact they had placed him under strict surveillance. A week before the local elections he was advised to resign and request his pension or take a vacation away from the city.

Instead, fearing for his children, he went to a nearby hospital and put them in the care of the director, who was still his friend. Adenauer also insisted on remaining in Cologne at his post. As a result, the Nazis decided to act. He was warned by a friend that on the Monday following election day, Stormtroopers would be awaiting him in his office. As soon as he arrived, they would throw him from a window. Adenauer took this warning seriously. He

Since Hitler is coming to Cologne not in his capacity as chancellor but as a speaker at a Nazi party election meeting, I see no reason why I, as lord mayor, should officially receive him.
—KONRAD ADENAUER
speaking on February 17, 1933

Maria Laach, a Benedictine monastery in the Eifel Hills near Belgium. Adenauer took refuge here in the summer of 1933, after the Nazis dismissed him as lord mayor of Cologne.

Adolf Hitler (1889–1945) addresses a Nazi party rally at Nuremberg in 1936. This gigantic meeting, carefully staged to convince Germany and the world of Hitler's irresistible power, is the subject of Leni Riefenstahl's controversial film *Triumph of the Will.*

asked for protection from the chief of police who had earlier told him that the police would "defend him to the last man." But now they refused to guarantee his safety.

Adenauer decided to go to Berlin and complain to the minister of the interior about conditions in Cologne. But first he had to make sure he would not be stopped by the Stormtroopers living in his house. In the early morning hours he slipped past the sleeping guard. He had instructed his wife to join the children at the hospital where he had sent them earlier, and had also told her to call and inform his secretary of his whereabouts. Then, he borrowed a car to drive to a nearby city, where he took a train to Berlin.

The minister of the interior, Hermann Göring, Hitler's chief lieutenant, listened to Adenauer and then accused him of having fled from Cologne with millions of marks from the city treasury. After Adenauer denied the accusation, Göring reminded him of the incident with the flags. The interview was over.

Adenauer was officially expelled from Cologne and forbidden to enter the city limits. His salary

Richard Strauss chats with leading Nazi Ernst Röhm (1887–1934) in 1933. Like millions of other Germans, the renowned composer blew with the prevailing political winds and followed Hitler's lead. He became president of the Chamber of State Music in 1933 but fell into disfavor with the Nazis in 1935 and went into retirement.

Hitler hounded political enemies like Adenauer, but Jews were the particular targets of his vicious policies. In 1936 he ordered a nationwide boycott of Jewish businesses. "Germans do NOT buy from Jews," reads this sign in a small, secluded Prussian town.

was stopped, and the Nazis refused to let him draw on his bank accounts. After being lord mayor for 16 years he began 12 years of exile from both his beloved city and political life.

Adenauer remained in Berlin and wrote his family every day. He went out rarely, not wanting to draw attention to himself. However, he did go to church as often as possible, where he renewed his faith in God.

His first concern was money, but this problem was solved unexpectedly. An American businessman who was a friend visited him and gave him 10,000 marks in cash. The man said it was an investment and refused to take an IOU, though he knew he might never be repaid. For one of the few times in his life Adenauer was speechless.

Adenauer at Maria Laach, where he remained for almost a year. The head of the monastery was his old friend Ildefons Herwegen.

Meanwhile, the threat of arrest grew. Adenauer's one friend at the *Gymnasium*, Ildefons Herwegen, had become the abbot of an 11th-century Benedictine monastery at Maria Laach in the mountains not far from Cologne. Adenauer went to him, and the abbot gave him sanctuary. Here Adenauer spent his time reading history and going for walks, though he had to be careful that no one saw him. During the summer his and Gussi's eldest son, Paul, visited him in the monastery and together they went for long walks. Paul later said that this time with his father was an important factor in his becoming a priest.

The Adenauers had always been a tight-knit family and as the holidays approached they missed this closeness. They decided to spend Christmas together at a hotel near the abbey. But since the family was large—Adenauer and his wife, the three grown children by his first wife and four younger ones by his second—there was the risk that someone would recognize them. And someone did. Shortly after the holidays the governor of the Rhineland warned the abbot against letting Adenauer stay. Although the abbot insisted he remain anyway, Adenauer, not wanting to cause his friend trouble, left.

Once more he went to Berlin, but this time his family joined him. To save as much money as possible, Adenauer began to sell the paintings he had collected over the years. A few months later, he was arrested for the first time.

When after a few days he was released, he went into hiding. For weeks he moved about, spending only a single day in any one place. He kept in touch with only his family and a few friends, one of whom suggested Adenauer find an out-of-the-way spot for himself and his family. Adenauer agreed and found a village called Rhöndorf, in the mountains overlooking the eastern bank of the Rhine River not far from Cologne.

But even here Adenauer was not safe. The *Gestapo*, or secret police, found him and plotted his murder. The plan failed only because they could find no one in Rhöndorf willing to kill him. Following this, the Nazis officially expelled him from the administrative area of Cologne, which included Rhöndorf. Thus he had to leave Rhöndorf and once more be separated from his family, which remained behind. He found a place four miles away and either his wife or one of his children visited him daily, making the trip by bicycle in all kinds of weather.

Life took an unexpected turn for the better when a new lord mayor took office in Cologne. He lifted the expulsion order and granted Adenauer's appeal for a pension. He also paid Adenauer for his two houses, which the city had taken over. The price was far below what the houses were worth, but Adenauer had the choice of taking it or contending with the wrath of the Gestapo. He took it.

Adenauer decided to use some of the money to buy some land in Rhöndorf on a steep hill overlooking the Rhine River, and there he built his last home. For once he was not thrifty. The house was spacious enough for the entire family, and graced with a garden and terrace large enough for him to spend countless hours indulging in his lifelong love of horticulture. The Adenauers lived quietly, seeing only a few old friends. It seemed that the Nazis had forgotten him.

In the summer of 1939 Adenauer could sense the imminence of war. Hitler had authorized a massive rearmament program shortly after becoming chancellor, and elements of the nation's armed forces had had a chance to test new methods of warfare during the Spanish Civil War (1936–1939). German troops and airmen had greatly contributed to the victory gained by the fascists under General Francisco Franco. Germany had also expanded its borders considerably since 1933. It had effected a political union with its German-speaking southern neighbor, Austria, in 1938. In 1939 Hitler's brutal diplomacy had also incorporated vast areas of Czechoslovakia into the German state.

Adenauer realized that Nazi Germany was about to dispense with diplomacy and that from now on political gains would be made by recourse to war. He took his wife to Switzerland for a few

Heinrich Himmler (1900–1945), head of the SS and chief of the Gestapo. As the élite guard of the Nazi party, the SS (*Schutzstaffel*) was responsible for most of the German atrocities committed during World War II. The Gestapo was the dreaded Nazi secret police.

Adenauer outside his house in Rhöndorf in 1938. He built the house in 1935 and lived there throughout the Hitler years, fearing arrest by the Gestapo at any time of day or night.

weeks, fearing that when hostility finally erupted the Gestapo might arrest everyone opposed to the war. And he was correct. By the time he returned, the first wave of arrests were over. One old friend had been arrested and was killed in a concentration camp. Adenauer later found out that his name had also been on the list of those to be rounded up, but for some reason had been crossed off. He never learned who had crossed it off or why.

As the war went on, life in Rhöndorf gradually changed. His older children had married and when his eldest sons went into the army, his daughters-in-law moved to Rhöndorf. Now the house was filled to overflowing. Adenauer was "Father Konrad," and his political skills undoubtedly helped calm the nerves of the many people in the house.

Adenauer had kept himself out of politics before the war, and he did the same during the war. Even though there were other Germans who hated Hitler as much as he did and who wanted to get rid of him, Adenauer did nothing to help overthrow him. One plot included several generals and politicians who had opposed Hitler before the war. One of the politicians was the former mayor of a city in eastern Germany. When Adenauer was asked to meet with him, Adenauer refused, later stating that he did not believe any plan led by the former mayor could succeed. In July 1944 the plot did fail. A bomb exploded during a conference between Hitler and his generals and only slightly wounded Hitler. The plotters were arrested, tried, and either killed or sent to prison. None survived the war.

A few days after Hitler's brush with death, the Gestapo arrived at the Adenauers. They searched the house, questioned Adenauer, and returned the next day, but did not arrest Adenauer. However, a month later he was taken to a concentration camp in the grounds of the Trade Fair Hall, which he himself had built. He was only one of many politicians and public officials who had been rounded up for opposing Hitler.

Hitler and some of his top army officers. In flagrant violation of the Versailles Treaty, Hitler built the German army into an effective and formidable fighting machine. His invasion of Poland on September 1, 1939, marked the official beginning of World War II.

Adenauer was befriended by the prisoner who ran the clothing depot. The man was a former communist who had served nine years at hard labor at another camp and had become a trusted worker at this camp. Because of this he was able to go into the camp office and check the daily lists of the prisoners who were being sent to death camps in Germany and the German-occupied territories of eastern Europe. When he saw Adenauer's name on a list he advised Adenauer to report sick. With the help of another prisoner, a physician, the plan worked.

The hospital where Adenauer was taken was the same hospital where he had sent his wife and children before he went to Berlin. Adenauer knew that sooner or later he would be sent back to the camp. He also knew he could probably escape, though this would cause trouble for the head of the hospital, an old friend. Just before he was to go back to prison, his wife enlisted the help of a

A British plane bombs a coal plant near Cologne in August 1941. That December the United States entered the war on the side of Britain and the Soviet Union, thus vastly increasing the weight of armed force arrayed against Germany.

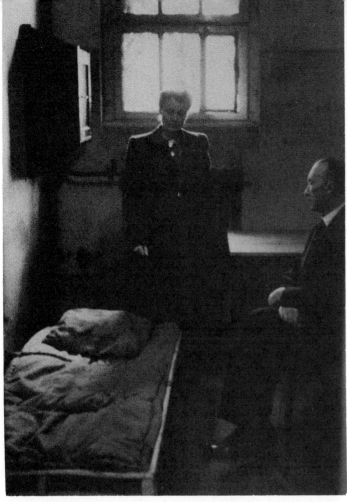

Adenauer's wife, Gussi, visits him in Brauweiler prison in 1944. Arrested after the unsuccessful attempt to assassinate Hitler in July of that year, Adenauer spent two months in Brauweiler. He was then 68 years old.

friend who was an air force officer. The officer went to the hospital and demanded that Adenauer be transferred to his custody for questioning in Berlin. Once again he was set free.

Adenauer went into hiding in the house of a miller in an isolated village. To protect his wife, he told her to go to the hospital to try to visit him and then go to the Rhöndorf police station to report him missing. The plan worked, but only for a few days. Just as Frau Adenauer thought she could relax she was arrested by the Gestapo, and when they threatened to arrest her two daughters she divulged her husband's location. After he was brought to the prison, she was released.

Cologne, like most of the major cities in Germany, was being heavily bombed in preparation for the advance of the American, British, and French armies. During one particularly heavy raid, both

Generals Dwight D. Eisenhower (1890–1969) and George S. Patton (1885–1945). Eisenhower (at left) was supreme commander of Allied forces in Europe. Patton commanded the U.S. Third Army in a brilliant drive from the Normandy beaches through France and across the Rhine into Germany (June 1944–March 1945).

If you continue to deny everything, Frau Adenauer, your husband must expect a very severe penalty; you will remain under arrest yourself, and I shall have your two daughters arrested today. And one thing I can promise you—they will stay down there in the cellar until we have got your husband, even if it takes months.

—Gestapo official to Adenauer's wife following her declaration that she knew nothing of her husband's whereabouts after his 1944 escape from the Nazis

the prisoners and their Gestapo guards took shelter in the basement. When Adenauer learned he was to be released in the morning, he insisted on leaving as soon as the raid was over. Since it was Sunday he could not get his belongings, and so, without a collar or tie or even shoe laces, he left.

During the next few months Adenauer and his family waited at Rhöndorf for the Americans to come. A storage cellar in a hill had been turned into an air raid shelter. When Rhöndorf was suddenly in the middle of a battle zone, all 14 members of his family—Adenauer, his wife, their three younger children, his older daughter and her two children, and his daughters-in-law and their children, and a young infant—moved into it. They were joined by five French escaped prisoners of war who had appeared one day asking for help. If the Gestapo had found them there, Adenauer would probably have been executed on the spot.

Battles were being fought all around them and over their heads. At the bottom of the garden, a German tank exchanged fire with American tanks across the Rhine River.

Every day, Adenauer went to a high spot overlooking the river to watch the progress of the Americans. One day the gunners in the American tanks saw him and turned their guns on the hill. Adenauer threw himself to the ground as shells exploded all around him. When the shelling let up, he went back to the air-raid shelter, dirty and temporarily deaf, but otherwise unharmed.

The battle continued for seven days. In addition to being shelled, the area was bombed. When one day Adenauer again hiked up to the top of the hill, he saw the American tanks and troops on the road below. As far as Rhöndorf was concerned, the war was over.

The Adenauers returned to their house, though it had not weathered the war as well as they had. Twelve direct hits from the shelling had destroyed the garage and the well, their only source of water, and the roof and walls of the house were damaged. The garden, Adenauer's pride and joy, was ruined.

Tanks of the U.S. Third Army roll into Cologne in 1945. After five years of war, Adenauer's beloved city was little more than rubble and ruins.

5

A Call to Duty

Adenauer did not have much time to put his own house in order. The day after his return, two American officers knocked on the door and asked for him.

Adenauer, wearing gardening clothes, asked what they wanted, and they replied that they wanted him to return to the post he had held 12 years earlier. If he agreed, he would be given all the authority necessary to help put his beloved native city back on its feet. But Adenauer could not agree. Though the war may have been over in Rhöndorf, it was not over for Germany. As long as Germany had not surrendered and his three sons were still fighting in the German army, he could not return to his old post. If he did, he would be accused of collaborating with the enemy, and his sons might have to pay with their lives.

The most he would agree to do was to work unofficially as an advisor. The Americans wanted Adenauer and were willing to accept his terms, and 15 minutes later Adenauer and his wife were on their way to Cologne. When they arrived, the Germans and the Americans were still fighting on the right bank of the Rhine. Adenauer and his wife moved into two rooms in a hospital, since their former residence was uninhabitable.

The job he faced was enormous. After World

An inmate of the Belsen concentration camp, April 1945. When the Allies marched into the camps, the full horror of Hitler's regime was revealed to the world. Those working to rebuild Germany after the war had to cope not only with physical devastation but with the moral shame of the Nazi atrocities.

In October 1945, after Cologne passed into the British occupation zone, Adenauer (at far left) was dismissed from office by the British commander, Brigadier John Barraclough (at far right). The stated reason was "inefficiency," but Adenauer suspected that Britain's socialist government had fired him because it considered his political views too moderate.

War I his biggest job had been to maintain order
and find food. He had had a staff, and people had
places to live. After World War II, however, Cologne
was in ruins and failed to supply even the most
basic human needs. Half of the city was completely
destroyed, and the rest of it, with the exception of
a mere 300 undamaged buildings, was barely hab-
itable. Streets had disappeared beneath mountains
of rubble, and the bridges that previously spanned
the Rhine River had been blown up, leaving the
city split in two. Cologne's desperate situation was
further aggravated by the fact that there was no
water, no electricity, and no gas.

To make matters worse, Adenauer had no
staff to help him, and the American occupation
authorities would not let him use the surviving
city employees since they were all former Nazis.
Before he could start to solve the city's problems,
he had to find people to assist him. Once more, he
used people's love of this city to unify both former
friends and political opponents who had not been
Nazis. "We owe it to Cologne," he said. "Cologne
needs you."

The rebuilding of the city was also hindered
by a lack of manpower. Though once there had
been 780,000 inhabitants in Cologne, the population had been reduced to only 32,000. However,
within days of the end of hostilities in the Rhineland thousands more returned from the country
and villages where they had found shelter during
the bombing and fighting. Most no longer had a
place to live.

Yet, hopeless as everything seemed, Adenauer
could not forget those people in the prison and
concentration camps who had done nothing to de-
serve their fate but disagree with Hitler and the
Nazis. As soon as the Germans were defeated and
the war was over on May 8, 1945, Adenauer sent
city buses to the concentration camps scattered
around Germany. The drivers found and brought
back only those prisoners who had once lived in
Cologne. "We owe it to these poor people," Adenauer said. One was the man who had shared his
room in the clothing depot with Adenauer at the

Trade Fair concentration camp.

All of these people had little or nothing to eat. Adenauer arranged with the occupation authorities to get some food from the American army depots. In addition he established a self-help organization, collecting any cars or trucks he could find and sending people out to the country to buy whatever food they could from the local farmers.

As the flow of returning people continued, the need for housing became desperate. Adenauer, however, did not start rebuilding immediately. His first step was to reunite physically both halves of

Cologne's Hohenzollern Bridge in 1945. Along with countless other structures, it was completely destroyed by Allied bombing. The cathedral also suffered extremely heavy damage.

British troops lead captured German officers to British lines to discuss surrender terms in May 1945. The Nazi defeat opened a new chapter in Adenauer's political career. Within days of taking Cologne, the Americans offered him his old post as lord mayor.

Cologne so food and supplies could come into the city from both sides of the Rhine River. He located the necessary steel and used it to repair bridges.

This decision displeased everyone, since people felt it was more important to use the steel to rebuild and repair their houses and factories. Despite the protests, Adenauer held firm, just as he had over the matter of the Green Belt after World War I. Meanwhile, he worked with architects on a new plan for the city.

Adenauer's appetite for work was as large as ever. He never turned away a visitor to his office nor was he ever distracted from his job of supervising the construction of the bridges, the feeding of the hungry, and the resurrection of his beloved city. During the reconstruction he was always forced to work with the American military government, for it still controlled the city. And winning the trust of the Americans was not easy. To the Americans, all Germans were Nazis or supporters of the Nazis and were responsible for starting the war and killing millions of Jews, Gypsies, and dissidents.

Adenauer, therefore, had to prove to the Americans that not all Germans were Nazis, and that he and other Germans could be trusted. But progress was slow. Just as the Americans began to trust him, Germany was divided into four zones of occupation: the Americans controlled the south, the British the Rhineland and Cologne, the French the west and southwest, and the Soviets the east.

In October the British ordered Adenauer to have the trees in the city cut down for firewood

Soviet premier Joseph Stalin (1879–1953), U.S. president Franklin D. Roosevelt (1882–1945), and British prime minister Winston Churchill (1874–1965) at the Teheran Conference in 1943. The "Big Three" met again at Yalta in 1945 to make arrangements for the occupation of Germany. As a result of these meetings, Germany was divided into four occupation zones, with the British, Americans, and French in the west and the Soviets in the east.

for the winter. But Adenauer refused. Once the trees were cut they were gone forever, and in addition he felt there were not enough trees to ease the fuel shortage. Instead, he suggested increasing the supplies of coal from the nearby mines. To illustrate the strength of his conviction he gave an interview to some American and British reporters. It was a bold move for a defeated German openly and publicly to criticize his conquerors.

The reporters asked him about the French suggestion of setting up an independent Rhineland. Adenauer rejected the idea. If Germany were carved up by the western Allies—the United States, Great Britain, and France—the Soviet Union would use that as an excuse to declare its zone the true Germany. Instead, Adenauer suggested the western Allies should work for one Germany. If that failed, he explained, then the three western zones should be politically united. Although no one could have known it at the time, that was exactly what was to happen four years later.

The British used Adenauer's refusal to cut down the trees as an excuse to dismiss him. However, there may have been another reason, one that had more to do with politics in Britain. Winston Churchill, the Conservative premier who led Britain's wartime coalition government, had been voted out of power, along with his party, in the national election of July 1945. The new Labor government was more sympathetic to the Social Democrats (SPD) than to men like Adenauer, lifelong members of conservative Catholic parties. The British expelled him from Cologne and told told him not only to keep out of politics altogether but also to have no further involvement in the "administration or public life" of Cologne and the entire British zone of occupation.

Adenauer returned to Rhöndorf and filed the British expulsion letter with the Nazi dismissal letter. Because of his opposition to the Nazis, that dismissal had not hurt him. However, he had always admired the British democratic way of life, and so he was deeply upset by their rejection.

Adenauer was almost 70 years old and his

For the first time, I felt the effect of Adenauer's personality upon me. His manner of speech was dry, matter-of-fact, and occasionally seasoned with biting irony, but his arguments invariably struck home. At the end of the interview I was no longer a Christian Socialist but secretary general of the CDU.
—JOSEPH LÖNS
speaking of his conversion to the Christian Democrat cause in 1946

wife was seriously ill in a hospital in Cologne. Other men of his age and background would perhaps simply have retired from politics, stayed home, and tended their roses. But not Adenauer. If he could not take part in politics in Cologne, he would do so in the French zone as a prelude to reentering political life at the national level.

That decision took courage, because all Germany was in ruins—physically, politically, and morally. After its defeat in World War II the country had been left an outcast among nations because of the atrocious crimes committed by Hitler and the Nazis.

Completely lacking a government it could call its own, Germany had been divided into four zones occupied by the Americans, British, French, and Soviets. And its capital, Berlin, was also divided

Field Marshal Wilhelm Keitel (1882–1946), the German army chief of staff, signs the instruments of surrender on May 8, 1945. Once the Germans had surrendered officially, Adenauer felt legally free to resume his duties as lord mayor of Cologne.

The ruins of the Krupp factory at Essen. The massive Krupp armaments company produced the bulk of Germany's military hardware during the war. The Allies had mixed feelings about allowing Germany to rebuild its industrial base. They wanted Germany to get back on its feet, but they did not want it to have the means to wage war.

into four sections, although it was situated deep inside the Soviet zone.

Like Cologne, many German cities had been devastated by Allied bombing. Almost 10 million Germans had died during the war. Millions of the survivors were wounded, widowed, and orphaned, and equally vast numbers of men were in prisoner-of-war camps in eastern Europe and the Soviet Union. Terrified by the prospect of living under Soviet occupation, hundreds of thousands of those who had lived in the east had fled to the western zones, thus aggravating an already desperate shortage of housing.

Food was being rationed at the rate of 1,000 calories per person per day—little relief to the hungry and malnourished. Germany's industry was being threatened with total collapse as the factories were shipped to other nations; cows were grazing where previously great industrial estates had dominated the landscape. The Germans themselves were confused and unsure of their future. The dictatorship under which they had lived for 12 years was gone, and they did not know where or to whom to turn.

Rebuilding the country, both physically and politically, would take courage and talent. The challenge in the political arena was enormous, since the government had to be rebuilt from scratch. A constitution with democratic values had to be written and political parties had to be organized. The memory of the Weimar Republic continued to cast a shadow over Germany's recent history—it had

American troops liberate the Dachau concentration camp in April 1945. One of Adenauer's first acts as lord mayor was to send municipal buses to the camps to collect imprisoned Cologne citizens and bring them home.

been the Weimar Republic with its supposedly perfect democratic constitution which had failed and paved the way for Adolf Hitler and the Nazi party. Adenauer and the other survivors were determined that history would not repeat itself.

Adenauer felt that Hitler had been able to take power because there had been too many political parties, all relatively small, with narrow interests and no real base of support. For this reason he did not want to revive his old Catholic Center party. Instead, he wanted a more broadly based party, founded on Christian ideals, which would appeal to Protestants as well as Catholics.

The result was the Christian-Democratic Union, or CDU, which Adenauer helped found. Because Adenauer could not go to Cologne, the first meeting of groups from all over Germany was held in Coblenz, a city near Cologne but within the

Hermann Göring (1893–1946), Hitler's right-hand man, consults his lawyer at the Nuremberg Trial. From 1945 to 1946, on the site of Hitler's vast 1936 rally, a British, French, Soviet, and American tribunal tried prominent Nazis on charges of genocide and violating the laws of war.

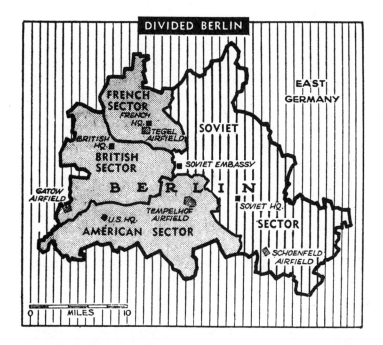

DIVIDED BERLIN

EAST GERMANY

FRENCH SECTOR

FRENCH HQ.

TEGEL AIRFIELD

SOVIET

BRITISH HQ.

BRITISH SECTOR

SOVIET EMBASSY

B E R L I N

GATOW AIRFIELD

TEMPELHOF AIRFIELD

U.S. HQ.

AMERICAN SECTOR

SOVIET HQ.

SECTOR

SCHOENFELD AIRFIELD

0 MILES 10

The four sectors of Berlin, former capital of the German Reich. With the war over and the Nazi menace gone, grave differences soon began to surface between the Soviet Union and the other occupying powers. Berlin, which lay deep in the Soviet zone, was a focal point for conflict.

French zone. When one meeting failed to start on time Adenauer preempted the official who had called it and took over as chairman. He said that he felt perfectly entitled to do so since he was the oldest person present. By the time the meeting was over he was elected permanent chairman and president.

During the next few years Adenauer put all his energies and talents into building a democratic Germany. The CDU grew as he traveled, made speeches, and met with others who believed as he did. Germany's future as a nation was being decided.

The first major step was taken a year after the end of the war when western Germany was divided into nine self-governing states, or "lands" (*Länder*), until a central federal government could be established. The Saar, an area rich in coal, located in western Germany bordering on France, was under French control. Its fate was to be determined later. Until there was a federal central government, the *Länder* were under the temporary control of the Allied high commissioners of the zones in which they were located—although no one was sure how long "temporary" was. Elections for

During the years of National Socialism the German people behaved in such a manner that I despised them. But since 1945 I have learned to feel some renewed respect for my people.
—KONRAD ADENAUER
speaking in 1946

the *Länder* governments were held in 1946.

As Adenauer had predicted when he was in the prison camp, Germany soon had to choose between the east and the west. In March 1948 the Soviet delegation walked out of a meeting of the four powers. The result was the year-long Berlin Blockade, during which the Soviets denied road access to the city from the west. Because of this the British, French, and Americans were forced to airlift food, fuel, and medicine to the people in their Berlin zones.

This example of Soviet intransigence persuaded the Allies to form a federal government in their zones, while simultaneously the Soviets formed a government of their own in their zone. The result was a democratic government in western Germany and a communist government in eastern Germany.

The 21 Nuremberg defendants listen as the verdicts are read on October 1, 1946. Three were acquitted, 7 received sentences of 10 years to life, and 11 were sentenced to death (including Hermann Göring, who committed suicide just before he was scheduled to hang).

The Berlin airlift. Tensions boiled over in Berlin in 1948 when the Soviet Union tried to expel Britain, France, and the United States by blockading the city. The Western nations thwarted the blockade by airlifting supplies into Berlin for more than a year.

In September 1948 a parliamentary council met in Bonn to draw up a constitution for West Germany. Adenauer was elected its president. In the meantime, however, personal tragedy had struck once more. In 1946 Adenauer's wife had had pneumonia from which she recovered, only to fall ill again. Finally, in March 1948, she died. Once more Adenauer spent the noon hour with his children, while the rest of his time was spent working.

The biggest task of his lifetime lay ahead of him. Once he had devoted himself to Cologne. Now he devoted his time, energy, and efforts to his country. To ensure that Germany would always have a stable government, Adenauer constantly reflected upon the Weimar experience. A key provision of the new government stated that the chancellor, or head of government, was to be elected by the

Bundestag, not directly by the voters, as in the United States. And now, before the *Bundestag* could dismiss a chancellor, it had to elect a new one. Thus, Germany would never be without a government.

Adenauer, of course, was not alone. He had the help of other men, all of whom wanted a democratic Germany. At the same time it was Adenauer, "the spokesman of the Federal Republic of Germany," who negotiated with the Allied authorities. The result of these deliberations was the Basic Law. It was to serve as the law of the land until all Germany was united, at which time a constitution was to be written. The military governments of the

These refugees were among tens of thousands who fled to West Germany after the Soviet Union established a communist state in the eastern part of the country. Though they aggravated the shortage of housing and food in the western sectors, Adenauer's government welcomed them.

three Western powers approved the Basic Law on May 8, 1949—four years to the day after Germany had surrendered.

Once the Basic Law was approved, West Germany had to have a capital, since Berlin, the former capital, was in East Germany. Because of its size, Frankfurt was the first choice. Adenauer objected on the grounds that the American military government was there. He suggested Bonn, a small city, famous for being the birthplace of the composer, Ludwig van Beethoven. Bonn was chosen, despite claims by critics that Adenauer wanted Bonn only because it was near his Rhöndorf home.

The next step in making West Germany a self-governing democracy was to hold elections for the *Bundestag*. Those elections were scheduled for August. The 72-year-old Adenauer campaigned with the energy of a man half his age.

A day of mourning for the victims of Nazism, September 14, 1947. Hitler's crimes hung like a dark shadow over the deliberations of the council charged with drafting a new constitution for Germany. As president of this council, Adenauer worked hard to design a system that would avoid the pitfalls of the Weimar Republic and prevent the rise of another dictator like Hitler.

Today I regard myself primarily as a European, and only in the second place as a German.
—KONRAD ADENAUER
speaking in 1946

6

A New Germany

When the *Bundestag* elections were over, Adenauer and the CDU had won the greatest number of seats, but they did not have a majority. To form a government and elect a chancellor, the leaders of the CDU needed to form a coalition or partnership with another party. To do this and to choose their candidate for chancellor, the leaders of the CDU and the CDU heads of the *Länder* met at Rhöndorf.

Adenauer, as host, claimed the chair. The CDU leader debated over which political party to ask to help form a government. Though Adenauer strongly favored a small party, and not the SPD, he let everyone have their say. Finally, he adjourned the meeting for supper—a cold buffet on the terrace in the garden, including a selection of fine wines from Adenauer's wine cellar. Afterwards, the guests were more relaxed, and the small party that Adenauer favored was quickly chosen to be asked to join the coalition.

The time had come to choose a chancellor, and someone proposed Adenauer. The former lord mayor of Cologne looked around, "as if surprised," one guest later remarked. Then he smiled and said, "If everyone agrees with this view, I accept. I've spoken to my doctor, and he has no objections. He even thinks I can carry on for two years."

Three weeks later the *Bundestag* met. As each deputy's name was called, he walked to the

When you fall from the heights as we Germans have done, you realize that it is necessary to break with what has been. We cannot live fruitfully with false illusions.
—KONRAD ADENAUER

Adenauer, accompanied by daughter Lotte, tends his garden at Rhöndorf. Many people believed that he fought so hard to have Bonn declared the capital of West Germany because Bonn was close to his beloved home. Nicknamed "Rose Gardener of Rhöndorf," Adenauer later had a rare species of rose named after him.

Chancellor Adenauer in front of the Palais Schaumburg, his official residence in Bonn. Nearly 80% of eligible voters took part in the 1949 election, giving Adenauer's Christian Democratic Union a narrow victory over their main opposition, the SPD.

rostrum and cast his ballot in one of the boxes. When the ballots were counted, Adenauer had won by one vote—just as he had in his last election for lord mayor of Cologne. He later told his youngest son, "Since I was determined to accept the appointment, I should have felt it sheer hypocrisy not to have voted for myself."

Adenauer became more than chancellor. He became entirely enmeshed in modern Germany's history—from that time on his life cannot be separated from the political life of West Germany.

The job ahead was a difficult one. Though West Germany had an elected government, it needed the permission of the three Allied powers to make laws and enforce them. The Allied military government, however, had transferred responsibility to diplomats or high commissioners who could veto German laws and determine Germany's foreign policy. As a result, Adenauer had to work and get along with the three different men from three different countries, each of which had different interests.

The Americans saw West Germany as a future ally against communism, and thus Adenauer quickly set up good relations with the American high commissioner, John J. McCloy, whose wife happened to be a distant relation to Adenauer's first wife. The British commissioner, Sir Brian Robertson, who was Catholic, became a friend as well. The French high commissioner was another matter. France had been invaded by the Germans twice in less than 30 years, and Adenauer sometimes needed the help of the British and American commissioners to win over the French commissioner.

An example of the problems Adenauer faced concerned the continuing influx of refugees. East Germans kept fleeing to the west. Some thought the Soviets were provoking the exodus in the hopes of making West Germany's economic problems so great that, unable to recover, it would remain weak and the Soviets could then take advantage of the situation. In fact, unemployment in western Germany was so high that two of the three high commissioners wanted to close the borders between east and west. However, Adenauer insisted on keeping the borders open and welcoming those Germans who had chosen to leave the Soviet zone.

The job that Adenauer faced as chancellor was threefold: firstly, Germany had to be rebuilt physically—its people needed housing, and its factories had to be put back into operation; secondly, Germany needed full sovereignty over its own affairs; and thirdly, after 12 years of a dictatorship that had seriously undermined moral values, the country needed a moral rebirth, both in the eyes of the Germans themselves and in the eyes of the rest of the world.

Despite the vast destruction, in many ways the first goal was the easiest. Though Adenauer was not an economist, other members of his party were. One must keep in mind that the collapse of Germany had been complete. Adenauer and the other members of his government were being given

Adenauer began rebuilding the Hohenzollern Bridge shortly after the war. Critics thought that the scarce materials should have been used for housing, but Adenauer argued that the bridge was vital for the transport of supplies.

a chance to decide Germany's fate. They wanted a free market system that incorporated a sense of social responsibility for the unemployed, the ill, the young, and the old. Its success depended on German industry's ability to provide the goods and the money.

Without the factories, any attempt at rebuilding or recovery was impossible. The Allies, however, were not eager to return to German ownership the large industrial plants that had been converted into tank, truck, and munition producers during the war. Adenauer had to fight for every factory and every machine.

He also had to please the people who had voted for him. Since he put the welfare of all Germans above the narrow considerations of party politics, his policies were not always popular with everyone. This was true of his solution to the problem of helping the refugees and other Germans

After World War II, many of Germany's former possessions in eastern Europe were given to Poland and the Soviet Union. In addition to the flood of refugees from East Germany, Adenauer's government found room for millions of German citizens displaced from these areas.

The ruins of Wesel, a port on the Rhine River about 50 miles north of Cologne, symbolize the enormous task of reconstruction faced by Adenauer and his government.

who had lost everything. In addition to the homeless in the west, there were the millions of refugees who had come from the east with nothing. However, amidst the poverty and suffering there were also Germans who made money during the war. Adenauer insisted that the wealthy Germans share with those who had none. He fought for a law, eventually passed in 1952, which provided for a heavy tax, as much as 50%, on the property of the wealthy. The collected money was redistributed to those who had lost everything.

The fate of the Saar Valley region still had to be decided. The French, who hoped to make it a part of France, had made it a separate district, outside the occupation zone. They had gone so far as to install their own civil government. Adenauer maintained that the Saarlanders themselves should choose the kind of government they preferred. He did not want to desert the Saarlanders who were German by origin and language, but he also recognized the need for France's friendship and its support for German sovereignty. And so he held his tongue. In the meantime, he worked hard for full sovereignty for West Germany.

Regardless of what German hard work could accomplish, full sovereignty, or self-rule, depended on the attitudes of the Allies. As the differences between east and west grew more pronounced, military and political partnership with the Allies began to seem absolutely crucial to Adenauer. The Berlin Blockade had marked the beginning of the "Cold War" between east and west—an ideological conflict that threatened to turn "hot" at any time. One result had been the creation of the North Atlantic Treaty Organization (NATO), a military and political alliance that embraced five European nations when first established in 1948 and then expanded to 12 members, including the United States, in 1949.

Though Germany was situated between France and the Soviet armies, Adenauer knew that if his country was attacked no western ally would hurry to defend Germany's freedom. As a result, he felt that a German military contribution to the defense of Europe would be a step toward full self-rule.

The European Defense Community (EDC), proposed by the French and supported by Ade-

Slowly but surely, Wesel rose from the ashes of war. During his first term as chancellor, Adenauer and his advisors began laying the foundation for the economic transformation of Germany from a land of ruins into a modern, competitive industrial nation.

Adenauer with British prime minister Winston Churchill on a state visit to Britain in December 1951. Adenauer basically disliked the British but needed their support in his campaign to make West Germany an equal partner with the other Western nations. Though Churchill greeted him warmly, a crowd of protesters shouting "Heil Hitler!" was proof that the bitter legacy of Nazism was not forgotten.

nauer and the leaders of other European countries, satisfied the American and, to a lesser degree, German pressure for a German rearmament, and also the European call for a more united European defense system. Adenauer insisted that the EDC would have to be tied to an agreement that would give Germany back its sovereignty. The Western armies could remain in Germany but not as armies of occupation.

If Adenauer was working for full self-rule for Germany, he was also working for Europe. In many respects, the man from Cologne was also one of the first Europeans. From almost the beginning of his first term, he worked for the idea of a European community. Under Adenauer's leadership the Federal Republic of Germany joined international organizations such as the World Bank and the International Monetary Fund, associations that would further lead Germany toward full self-government and responsibility for foreign affairs. This also helped carry West Germany back into the fold of civilized nations.

All of these factors led to a moral rebirth of Germany. But there was one more factor that re-

We are at all times ready to live in peace with our Eastern neighbors, especially with the Soviet Union and Poland. It is our urgent wish to see the present tensions between the Soviet Union and the Western Allies find their solutions in the course of time in a peaceful manner.
—KONRAD ADENAUER

Jews wearing the Star of David in Hitler's Germany. Under Adenauer, Germany made payments to Jewish survivors of Nazism. He knew that money could never compensate them, but he considered it a symbol of German resolve never to forget and never to repeat the crimes of Hitler. A reparations agreement was concluded in 1953.

We are certain that the narrow conception of the nation state ... has today altogether outlived its validity. From it arose nationalism in all its forms, and this brought the break-up and fragmentation of European life. If we are to find our way back to the sources of our European cultural heritage which has its fountain-head in Christian beliefs, we must succeed, first of all, in reestablishing the unity of the European way of life in all its apsects.
—KONRAD ADENAUER

quired serious attention. Adenauer felt that in some way the Jewish survivors of Hitler's persecution had to be compensated. Although money could never atone for the deaths, torture, and suffering, it could provide much-needed support and assistance for those Jews who were now struggling to rebuild their lives and communities. Once again, Adenauer had to fight for what he believed. A few West Germans resisted, feeling that Hitler, not they, had been responsible, and some Jewish groups rejected any German offer of peacemaking and conciliation. In the end, Adenauer had his way, and reparations were made to Jewish families that had lost family or possessions during the Holocaust.

Adenauer's hopes for the EDC and the Germany Treaty that would end the Allied occupation were constantly being postponed. France's fears about rearming Germany had to be overcome. Adenauer insisted that the two agreements had to be tied together, although Britain and the United States were not in the EDC. Finally, in 1952, the Germany Treaty was signed by representatives of the Allies and the EDC was signed by the French.

Now came the struggle to get the agreements passed by the legislatures of the countries involved. The U.S. Congress promptly signed the Germany Treaty, as did the British. In both Germany and France, the struggle took much longer. But both houses of the German parliament finally signed them in the spring of 1953.

Shortly afterwards, Adenauer became the first German chancellor ever to go to the United States. The first day of the momentous trip was spent in New York—and one of Adenauer's first visits was to the man who had given him the money in Berlin so many years before. While in Washington, D.C., he visited Arlington National Cemetery and the Tomb of the Unknown Soldier. "It was," he said, "one of the most beautiful and moving things I have ever experienced."

Adenauer at Arlington National Cemetery on April 8, 1953. Surrounded by the graves of Americans who had died fighting Germany, he laid a wreath at the Tomb of the Unknown Soldier. Adenauer later came to consider the event a landmark in the endeavors of the United States and Germany to replace their former enmity with a measure of reconciliation.

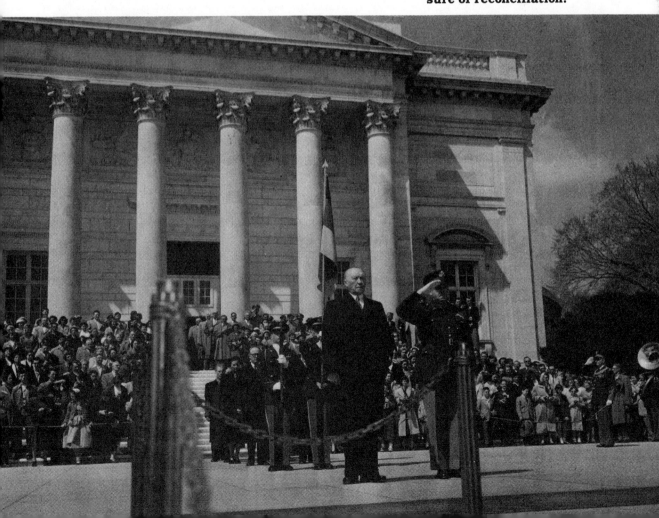

The workers of East Berlin march against their Soviet-backed communist government on June 17, 1953. The uprising, which quickly spread throughout East Germany, was savagely crushed by Soviet tanks. In its wake, Adenauer was more determined than ever to make West Germany a bulwark against communism.

By the time Adenauer returned home, the people of East Germany had revolted against their Soviet occupiers. The rising was easily and brutally suppressed by Soviet military forces. Soviet dictator Joseph Stalin's claim to have established a "people's democracy" in East Germany stood revealed as nonsense. Adenauer immediately went to Berlin. Although he was in no position to offer practical support to the East Berliners, he showed both East and West Germany that he cared for those Germans who were under the totalitarian rule of the Soviet Union. He voiced the hope that some day the East Germans would be as free to vote for their choice of government as the West Germans. At the same time, the true outlines of both the fate and shape of Europe were now readily apparent.

That fall the West Germans again went to the polls to vote in national elections to the *Bundestag* and thus decide which party would select the chancellor who was to lead them for another four years. Adenauer and his CDU party campaigned on the strength of their achievements: they had signed an agreement that would terminate the Allied occupation within two years; they had reduced unemployment to levels almost unprecedented in a modern industrial nation; they had built almost 2 million new homes; they had increased agricultural production; and they had raised the standard of living.

Adenauer and the CDU won by a large majority, and Adenauer was elected chancellor by a majority of 101. Known as *Der Alte*, the Old One or the Old Man, both because of his age and as a title of respect, Konrad Adenauer had emerged as the most important man in the political life of postwar Germany.

> *Are not we Germans, who bear so much guilt as a result of the war, under an obligation now to devote all our intellectual, moral, and economic strength to the task of making this Europe an element of peace?*
> —KONRAD ADENAUER

Adenauer on the campaign trail in the fall of 1953. In September his Christian Democratic Union won a resounding victory at the polls, and the 77-year-old chancellor was elected to a second term.

7

Der Alte

When Adenauer was sworn in for his second term as chancellor, West Germany was a different place than it had been four years earlier. He had led the way toward the "economic miracle" that was transforming the country.

The cities were being rebuilt, industry was booming, and employment was at record levels. The products for whose quality Germany had been world famous before the war were once more leaving the factories. Leica cameras and Mercedes-Benz cars were available again and had lost none of their power status symbols. Then there was the Volkswagen, the automobile first sanctioned by Adolf Hitler as a "people's car." Although a few had been built during the 1930s, this rugged and inexpensive machine had all but disappeared once the factory that made it changed over to war production. Now, however, the factory returned to manufacturing the little car, called the beetle, and VWs, as they were known, rolled off the assembly lines at a price both Germans and the world could afford.

While Germany's economic situation was improving, several major political problems remained. Allied occupation in every form was due to end in two years, but the French parliament still had not voted on the EDC pact that would bring West Germany fully into the European community. And the Saarland was still controlled by France. There was also the question of the Soviet Union.

Adenauer in 1957, the year he was elected to a third term as chancellor. His margin of victory was even larger than in 1953.

A coal mine near the Rhine port of Gelsenkirchen. Under Adenauer, German industry prospered by utilizing the best available technologies.

At the time of the uprising of June 17, 1953, in East Berlin, Adenauer had called for free elections in East Germany and an eventual reunification of the entire country. He had already taken a defiant stand against the Soviets, as was evident in the tone of his speeches and his constant expressions of sympathy for those Germans under Soviet occupation. The Soviets, however, attempted to defuse this situation by offering to discuss the possibility of concluding a peace treaty that would officially end World War II. Such a treaty would, they hoped, keep West Germany out of NATO, the alliance that had been formed to defend Western Europe against any Soviet aggression. Both Adenauer and the western Allies rejected the offer.

Adenauer, meanwhile, was still hoping that the French parliament would approve the European Defense Pact, calling for a European army with German participation. The French, however, faced serious political problems of their own, with no one man able to form a government or govern for long. As a result, Adenauer urged that the Basic Law be amended to permit West Germany to create an army that would serve within NATO.

The idea of a new German army was not popular. Few people had forgotten the German army that had crushed Europe and had, in turn, been crushed itself. Adenauer had to fight hard for the change. The opposing Social Democrats, for example, felt that West Germany's top priority should be reunification. Adenauer finally won, however, and the Basic Law was changed. But he was never to get his wish for a European army, since the French parliament voted against it in August 1954.

On May 9, 1955—10 years after World War II ended—West Germany joined NATO and on the same day resumed control of its foreign affairs. West Germany was thus placed firmly within the Western camp. A few months later Adenauer accepted a Soviet invitation to go to Moscow.

Adenauer had consistently proposed that a forceful policy of German rearmament and solid commitment to NATO would eventually persuade the Soviets to allow the reunification of Germany.

A Volkswagen assembly line. By the mid-1950s Germany's economy was going strong. The country's speedy and substantial transition from devastation to industrial predominance came to be known as the "economic miracle."

Unfortunately, the Soviets were scornful of his position and insisted that the Federal Republic agree to diplomatic recognition of the Soviet Union before any discussion of their releasing the 10,000 German prisoners of war still held in the Soviet Union. Adenauer's acceptance of the Soviet terms caused a storm of protest in West Germany and the rest of Europe, where many people felt that recognition of the Soviet Union would give the Soviet occupation of East Germany a measure of legitimacy. If the trip to Moscow was unpopular with West Germans who had relatives in East Germany, the return of 10,000 Germans from prison camps went some way toward making up for it. By the end of the year, trains filled with the former prisoners were arriving in the west.

In 1957 the question of the status of the Saarland was finally settled. One of Adenauer's goals was friendship with France, but he had insisted that the German Treaty have a provision for the Saarlanders to vote to unite with either France or Germany. After the failure of the EDC, Adenauer began to urge the French to allow the Saarlanders to vote. The vote was finally held, perhaps because the French believed the Saar would vote to join France. If the vote had been held a few years after the war, the Saarlanders might have voted for France. But instead, the Saarlanders voted to rejoin Germany and become a part of the German "economic miracle."

That same year, Germany, France, Italy, Belgium, the Netherlands, and Luxembourg formed the European Economic Community (EEC). Its goal was to remove trade barriers and travel restrictions between and among European countries. Adenauer was one of its strongest advocates. A Europe united in such a way, he felt, would be united for peace, not war. There would be no reason for war among countries so joined for the common good. It was a

Nikita Khrushchev (1894–1971), Soviet premier from 1958 to 1964. When Adenauer went to Moscow in 1955, Khrushchev was already the dominant figure in the post-Stalin Soviet government. The two men disliked one another intensely and traded accusations about which army, the German or the Soviet, had committed the greater atrocities during the course of World War II.

Adenauer prays at a Catholic church in Moscow in 1955. During this trip, he made one of the most difficult decisions of his career—to establish diplomatic relations with the Soviet Union. He hoped to open the way to talks on the reunification of Germany. In fact, by recognizing the Soviet Union, he recognized the East German Soviet puppet state.

step toward realizing Adenauer's dream of a Europe where people would consider themselves not just citizens of a particular nation but European too.

During these years, Adenauer served his country well. Even his longtime rivals, the Social Democrats, had to concede that the West German economy was booming. There was so much work for everyone that "guest workers" from Italy, Greece, Turkey, and other countries were welcome and necessary. The German people responded by again electing Adenauer and the CDU in 1957. Despite Adenauer's efforts, relations with France remained strained. The French still distrusted the Germans who had invaded their country twice in the space of 21 years. In addition, France was going through the same rapid change of governments that had troubled the Weimar Republic. As a result, Adenauer had been unable to form any kind of working relationship with a French head of state. That changed in 1958 when the French asked their wartime leader, General Charles de Gaulle, to take over the government.

Adenauer went to France to meet the general. However, he was not impressed by de Gaulle when he visited him at his home in Colombey-les-Deux-Eglises. Adenauer was practical by nature, an experienced politician who believed in down-to-earth politics. Though they shared a dream of a new Europe, Adenauer disapproved of de Gaulle's mystical sense of mission, his dramatic gestures, and his very militaristic character.

By 1962, however, the two men had achieved a partial reconciliation. Problems were still to arise,

Adenauer with Charles de Gaulle (1890–1970) in 1961. After de Gaulle became the French head of state in 1958, Adenauer stepped up his efforts to improve French-German relations. Both men were strong personalities with autocratic tendencies, but they managed to cooperate on those occasions when their interests coincided.

especially over the establishment of NATO and over whether Great Britain should join the EEC—Adenauer was in favor of both, while de Gaulle opposed them. The much-improved relations between France and Germany—and de Gaulle and Adenauer—resulted in their signing the Franco-German Treaty of Friendship in 1963. That same year, de Gaulle led the way in refusing to allow Great Britain to join the European Economic Community. If Adenauer did not feel that Great Britain was "European-minded," most West Germans disagreed. A treaty of friendship with Britain, they felt, would have been as appropriate as one with France. By then, however, Adenauer was already having political problems both inside and outside the CDU.

Adenauer remained firmly in charge, both as chancellor of Germany and leader of the CDU. He

In October 1954, in the midst of complex negotiations about the European Defense Community and the fate of the Saarland, Adenauer took time off to accept an honorary degree from Columbia University in New York. There he met Britain's Queen Mother Elizabeth, who was also awarded a degree.

De Gaulle paid a state visit to Germany in September 1962. In Bonn he and Adenauer were cheered by crowds with bilingual signs calling for a united Europe. Touring the country, de Gaulle gave his speeches in German and was greeted with wild and heartfelt enthusiasm.

was admired and respected at home and abroad. Although he was in his 80s he did not even consider retiring. His only rival in the CDU was Ludwig Erhard, the economist whom he had brought into the government in 1949. In fact, it was Erhard, with his theories of the "market economy," who was most responsible for West Germany's economic recovery. Many Germans assumed that Erhard would be Adenauer's successor.

When, in 1959, the largely ceremonial job of president had been vacant, Adenauer had proposed Erhard for the presidency. This would have removed Erhard from being in line for chancellor. When that failed, he suggested himself and then changed his mind. This indecisiveness damaged Adenauer's reputation.

Though West Germany was booming, East Germany was not. East Germans who left East Germany—and many did—were welcomed into the west. To stop the flood, the Soviets and the East German government closed the border between the two Germanies. To make that border even more visible and impassable, they put up a wall, which consisted mostly of barbed wire at first. The Allies remembered the Berlin airlift and were determined

Adenauer, President Eisenhower, and Vice-President Nixon (at left; 1913–   ) in Washington, D.C., in 1960. Adenauer had an excellent working relationship with the Eisenhower administration but did not get along with Eisenhower's successor, John F. Kennedy (1917–1963), whom he described as "a cross between a junior naval person and a Roman Catholic boy scout."

In August 1961 the East German communist regime strung barbed wire between the two sectors of Berlin. Within days the barbed wire became bricks and mortar—the Berlin Wall, built to keep the people of East Germany prisoners in their economically troubled, harshly repressive country.

to guarantee their right of access to Berlin through East Germany. They sent troops to the highway checkpoints.

Adenauer did not react to the wall or the threat to Berlin. Unlike the time of the June 17 uprising, he did not go immediately to Berlin to reassure the Berliners. One reason may have been that the mayor of West Berlin was the leader of the SPD and thus a political rival. In any event, many people felt that his inaction on this occasion exhibited bad judgment. In August 1961 the wall became bricks and mortar, a permanent and visible reminder of the division between the former capital and the former nation.

Despite these events the West Germans were well off under Adenauer and the CDU. When elections were held in 1961, not long after the Berlin

In March 1962 President Kennedy sent his brother Robert (1925–1968) to Germany to discuss U.S.-German relations. During his visit, Robert Kennedy placed a wreath on a memorial to an East German killed while trying to escape to West Berlin.

Wall was erected, Adenauer was reelected along with the CDU, but the CDU did not gain a majority. Adenauer had to rely on other parties in order to form a government. Before, he had been able to form very quickly the cabinet that was necessary for a chancellor to govern. This time he needed 51 days to form a coalition. Even then, he had to promise to resign before the end of his term.

In 1962 the *Spiegel* affair exploded in the face of German democracy—and even Adenauer failed to come out of this disaster smelling like a

An aerial view of the Berlin Wall, 1962. At first only several feet high, the wall grew to a 12-foot fortified barricade. Desperate East Germans still tried to escape by sneaking over it, tunneling under it, or crashing through it, and many died in the attempt.

rose. The German magazine *Spiegel* had been critical of Adenauer's policies for some time and had printed an article blaming government defense policy for the German army's indifferent performance in NATO maneuvers. Adenauer then approved blatantly unconstitutional, occasionally rough police tactics during the investigation as to whether or not *Spiegel* had endangered state security by digging up the information and then publishing it. When Adenauer's cabinet resigned in the face of mounting public protest, he had six weeks in which to form another government—and only on the promise to resign the chancellorship in the autumn of 1963.

Actually, he served less than half that time. The CDU, which he had led for so long, elected

Erhard his successor as leader of the party. Adenauer was all alone. He resigned both as chancellor and as a member of the *Bundestag*. For the last time, Konrad Adenauer went home to Rhöndorf.

His time as chancellor had been longer than that of any of the Weimar Republic's 21 chancellors and longer than the actual duration of the "Thousand Year *Reich*" (labeled as such by Hitler, who fully believed his Third Reich would last a thousand years), which had come between the Weimar Republic and his chancellorship. He was now 87.

Adenauer with his successor, Chancellor Ludwig Erhard (1897–1977), formerly minister of economics. Adenauer disliked Erhard and did little to prepare him for his new, critically important job.

8

The End of the Long Road

At long last Adenauer could devote himself to his garden, growing roses, as he had dreamed of doing in his youth, instead of continuing to help West Germany consolidate its fledgling democracy. And he did spend many hours in his garden. He was also surrounded by his family. Every Sunday his sons and his daughters and their children gathered at Rhöndorf.

But he could not rest peacefully. In addition to writing his memoirs he bitterly criticized his successor. Though Ludwig Erhard was not a great chancellor, he had worked hard to maximize Germany's economic performance and keep the "economic miracle" on track. Indeed, since Adenauer had done little to train Erhard for the job of chancellor, his constant criticism of Erhard was a reflection of his own failings.

Adenauer also traveled, one of his last trips occurring in 1966. Still healthy at age 90, Adenauer went to Israel where he met with one of the founders of the state of Israel, David Ben-Gurion. As early as 1952 Adenauer had suggested establishing diplomatic relations between the two countries, but Israel, haunted by memories of the terrible Nazi era had not wished to consider such a move at that time. But this had not prevented Adenauer from continuing to seek a special arrangement with

Adenauer in retirement. He was 87 when he stepped down as chancellor of the Federal Republic of Germany, a post he had held for 14 years.

The German government held a grand celebration for *Der Alte* on the occasion of his 90th birthday, January 5, 1966.

Israel. Although he had had nothing to do with the Nazi crimes against the Jews, his conscience had led him to try to help atone for the sake of all Germans. This trip and the meetings with Ben-Gurion and Prime Minister Levi Eshkol constituted a historic event that served to emphasize Adenauer's hopes for an understanding between West Germany and Israel.

A year later Adenauer began to feel the weight of his 91 years and started to put his affairs in order. One by one his children and grandchildren came to his bedside. When they would start to cry he had the strength to point to the picture over his bed—a painting of God holding Jesus—and say, "No reason for crying."

On April 19, 1967, Konrad Adenauer died. The funeral was held in Cologne Cathedral, where President de Gaulle of France, President Lyndon B. Johnson of the United States, and the leaders of many other countries from all over the world came to pay their respects to a great German and a great man.

Adenauer's life was extraordinary in bridging nearly the entire history of modern Germany. Born only a few years after Germany was united

The historic meeting between Adenauer and David Ben-Gurion (1886–1973) at New York's Waldorf-Astoria Hotel in March 1960. The German chancellor and the Israeli prime minister established a warm, respectful relationship at this meeting. In 1966, at age 90, Adenauer traveled to Israel for a final meeting with Ben-Gurion.

under the *Kaiser*, he grew up in the conservative and militaristic *Kaiserreich*; his political life bridged the last years of Germany's imperial period and the turmoil of the Weimar Republic; he was driven from office, imprisoned, and made to suffer under the "Thousand Year Reich" of Adolf Hitler; and he helped create and then led the Federal Republic of Germany.

Adenauer found within himself the courage, ability, and dedication that was essential to the moral and material restoration of Germany. He was not afraid to act as spokesman for the conscience of his country when millions throughout the world considered it not just an outcast among nations but beyond all hope of redemption.

He had an immense capacity for learning and continued to accumulate knowledge all his life. What he had learned as lord mayor of Cologne following World War I, for example, proved invaluable to him when he shouldered the responsibility of supervising the resurrection of his tattered home-

After his death, Adenauer's house at Rhöndorf was turned into a memorial and an archive.

land in the aftermath of World War II.

One of his greatest political strengths was that he knew how to appeal to both friend and foe, and throughout his career he was consistently successful in persuading them to work together for the good of the majority of people. He had a generosity of spirit that enabled him both to accept the guilt for crimes that others had committed and compensate the victims.

Konrad Adenauer had a deep, abiding belief in God, and his lifelong religious convictions sustained him throughout trials and tribulations that might have crushed a lesser man. When he set out to do something, he did not stop until he had reached his goal.

And yet this solid faith in his abilities had its negative side—sometimes he was blind to all points of view other than his own. His unyielding determination to see a suspension bridge built across the Rhine at Cologne had almost cost him his job as lord mayor. And much later, his unwillingness to relinquish the chancellorship of the Federal Republic of Germany caused unnecessary and destructive turmoil in the country that he had helped to create.

When judged on his first two or two and a half terms as chancellor, he can be considered a giant among men. Even after 1959, when he undoubtedly made several serious miscalculations and persisted in refusing to retire, he was, in many ways, simply keeping faith with his own personal and political beliefs. He felt Germany could not survive without him, and acted like a father afraid to let his child take its first few steps alone. And yet, in the first analysis, the government and the democracy he had helped create were stronger than he was—perhaps stronger than he cared to admit.

Konrad Adenauer was a remarkable leader whose best instincts had been formed by all that was best about his country's past. It was as a true German that he helped his countrymen recover from the nightmares of the Nazi era and the devastation they had suffered. They had been led astray by amoral politicians who pretended to speak for

Germany yet offered nothing to the world but genocide and total war. Throughout that terrible period Konrad Adenauer kept alive the torch of decency, honesty, and humanity. He led Germany out of the darkness of unthinking nationalism and into the light of a wider concept of international cooperation. Had he never come to prominence, Europe might not have become the stable and forward-looking community of nations that it is today.

Adenauer was buried at Rhöndorf next to his first wife, Emma, his second wife, Gussi, and his son Ferdinand, Gussi's first child, who died in infancy.

Further Reading

Berghahn, V. R. *Modern Germany: Society, Economy, and Politics in the Twentieth Century.* Cambridge: Cambridge University Press, 1982.

Craig, Gordon A. *The Germans.* New York: G. P. Putnam's Sons, Inc., 1982.

Hiscocks, Richard. *The Adenauer Era.* New York: J. B. Lippincott Company, 1966.

Holborn, H. *A History of Modern Germany.* Princeton, New Jersey: Princeton University Press, 1982.

Laqueur, Walter. *Europe Since Hitler.* New York: Penguin Books, 1983.

Weymar, Paul. *Konrad Adenauer.* London: Andre Deutsch, 1957.

Chronology

Jan. 5, 1876	Born Konrad Adenauer, in Cologne, Germany
1901	Passes second state law examination, thus achieving rank of assistant judge
Jan. 1904	Marries Emma Weyer
March 7, 1906	Elected deputy mayor of Cologne
1909	Elected first deputy mayor of Cologne
Aug. 1914	Germany goes to war against France, Russia, and Great Britain
Oct. 16, 1916	Death of Emma Adenauer
Oct. 18, 1917	Adenauer is elected lord mayor of Cologne
Nov. 11, 1918	Armistice brings World War I to an end
Sept. 25, 1919	Adenauer marries Auguste ("Gussi") Zinsser
March 1933	Dismissed from office by the Nazis
1944	Imprisoned and released by the Nazis
March 1945	Reinstated as lord mayor of Cologne by American occupation authorities
May 8, 1945	Germany's unconditional surrender to the Allies brings the war in Europe to a close
Oct. 6, 1945	Adenauer dismissed from office by British military government
1946–49	Adenauer establishes the Christian Democratic Union party and helps devise the Basic Law, Germany's new constitution
Sept. 17, 1949	Adenauer is elected chancellor of the Federal Republic of Germany
June 17, 1953	Population of East Germany rises against its Soviet-backed government
Oct. 9, 1953	Adenauer is reelected chancellor
1955	The Federal Republic of Germany becomes a sovereign state
1961	Adenauer is elected to a fourth term as chancellor
Oct. 11, 1963	Adenauer resigns the chancellorship
1966	Visits Israel
April 19, 1967	Adenauer dies, of natural causes, at his home in Rhöndorf

Index

Edythe Cudlipp has written numerous books and magazine articles on a variety of subjects, including fashion, women's issues, medicine, and international advertising. She became interested in German history, and especially the Adenauer era, during the seven years that she spent in West Germany as a civilian editor with the U.S. Army. Ms. Cudlipp lives and works in New York City.

Arthur M. Schlesinger, jr., taught history at Harvard for many years and is currently Albert Schweitzer Professor of the Humanities at City University of New York. He is the author of numerous highly praised works in American history and has twice been awarded the Pulitzer Prize. He served in the White House as special assistant to presidents Kennedy and Johnson.